LIFE ISSUES

RACISM

by Scott Hays

Marshall Cavendish

NEW YORK • LONDON • TORONTO • SYDNEY

Published by Marshall Cavendish Corporation
2415 Jerusalem Avenue
North Bellmore, New York 11710
USA

Library of Congress Cataloging-in-Publication Data

Hays, Scott Robert.
    Racism / Scott Hays.
       p. cm. — (Life issues)
    Includes bibliographical references and index.
    ISBN 1-85435-687-9 (set). — ISBN 1-85435-615-1
    1. Racism—Juvenile literature. [1. Racism. 2. Prejudices.]
I. Title. II. Series.
HT1521.H39 1994   93-40422
305.5—dc20   CIP
                               AC

Produced by The Creative Spark
Editor: Gregory Lee
Art direction: Robert Court
Design: Mary Francis-DeMarois, Robert Court
Page layout, graphic illustration: Mary Francis-DeMarois

Marshall Cavendish editorial director: Evelyn M. Fazio
Marshall Cavendish editorial consultant: Marylee Knowlton
Marshall Cavendish production manager: Ruth Toda

Printed and bound in the United States of America

Author's Note
With the exception of the researchers and experts who were quoted in this book, all names have been changed to protect the identities of those people who were willing to be interviewed.

Photographic Note
Several persons depicted in this book are photographic models; their appearance in these photographs is solely to dramatize some of the situations and choices facing readers of the Life Issues series.

Photo Credits
Bettmann Newsphotos: 10 (UPI); 56 (Reuters)
Big Brothers/Big Sisters of America: 4 (John Reeves); 84 (Claire Lewis)
Christie Costanzo: 55
The Image Works: 6 (Nita Winter); 36 (Wells); 41 (M. Antman); 46 (Katherine McGlynn); 74 (Michael J. Okoniewski)
Impact Visuals: 18 (Rick Reinhard); 24, 28, 58 (Marilyn Humphries); 29, 64 (Harvey Finkle); 32 (Hilary Marcus); 69 (Catherine Smith); 78 (Clark Jones); 82 (Hazel Hankin)
Jeroboam, Inc.: 22 (Laima Druskis)
Magnum Photos: 9 (Danny Lyon); 51 (Eli Reed); 62, 67, 71, 87 (Paul Fusco)
PhotoEdit: 44 (M. Richards); 48 (Robert Brenner); 53 (Paul Conklin); 80 (Mary Kate Denny)
Photo Researchers, Inc.: 12, 16 (Kathy Sloane); 39 (Kenneth Murray); 76 (Roberta Hershenson)

Cover photo Jeroboam, Inc. (Arnold J. Saxe)

Acknowledgments
Editorial consultant: Judith Wilson, Executive Director, Yonkers Community Action Program, Yonkers, New York

TABLE OF CONTENTS

Prologue 5

1 In the Company of Racism 7
What Is Racism? • Class and Ethnic Racism • Why Do
We Invent Stereotypes? • Years of Schooling • Is There
Some Racism in All of Us? • Racism Often Begins at Home

2 On the Front Lines 23
Confronting Racism • One Teacher's Approach
• Caught in the Middle • The Problem Is Skin Deep

3 Crossing the Color Barrier 37
Discovering Your Roots • Ethnic Pride • Making the
Connection • Tearing Down the Walls • Watch What You Say

4 When Hate Turns Violent 49
A Disturbing Picture • Hate Groups • The Los Angeles Riots
• For Better or Worse • Can We All Get Along?

5 Racism in School 65
Multiculturalism • What About Teachers? • Racism in Sports
• The Great Equalizer • It Takes Teamwork • Affirmative Action

6 Face the Hate 81
It's Never Easy • Reducing Resistance • Classroom Techniques
For Change • What's Next? • Learn to Help Each Other

Additional Resources 90
For Further Reading 92
Glossary 93
Index 95

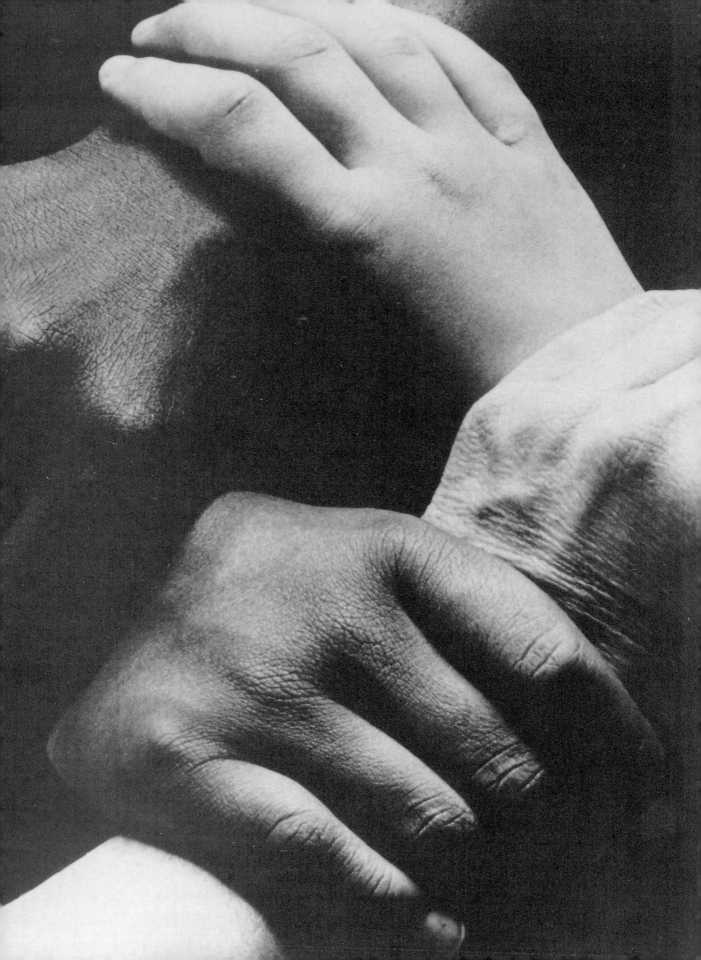

Prologue

Recognizing racism can be a painful process. Hearing the stories of people whose lives have been changed by hate crimes, discrimination, or a racial slur isn't pleasant. Coming to grips with your own views about different races and cultures is also difficult at times. Exploring these feelings and attitudes is important, however, because it provides useful insight into your relations with the other people around you.

What is racism? If you make a joke about the color of a person's skin, does that make you a bigot? Is racism learned or are we born with it? Why do some of us hate people who are different? How do we overcome our prejudices?

Chances are you've encountered racism. Maybe you've seen graffiti on a wall that mocks someone else's race. Maybe you've made negative remarks against another group of people. You may even have friends who belong to a gang that promotes hate. Racism is not necessarily about a few bigoted individuals who simply do not know any better. It is a set of ideas and practices that result in negative treatment of members of a racial or ethnic group.

Most young people today have experienced, seen, or heard about an incident of racial violence. Strong emotions like fear and hate come easy to some members of our society. No community is immune. No one is blameless.

Whether you've been the victim of a hate crime, the target of a racial slur, or the one doing the discriminating, this book will help you better understand the causes and realities of racism as it exists in everyday life. One note of caution: Offensive words or phrases may be used as illustrations that may generate emotional responses as you read. These may range from guilt and shame to anger and despair. However, try not to let your emotions get the better of you. To understand an opposing viewpoint, we must sometimes consider and analyze the positions of those with whom we disagree, even though we may find it distasteful or disagreeable.

According to census figures released in 1992, the United States admitted 8.6 million immigrants, more than in any decade since 1900-1910. This change in the composition of the American public could mean a bumpy ride for some of you who will have to confront the issues of race and racism. One way to smooth over the rough spots is through education. Your paths as members of different groups forming one society are crisscrossing every day. You can choose to either learn from and be open to new cultures and new ideas while still respecting your own, or reject them and miss out on new possibilities.

The search for truths about racism in any society is a painful process, but we sometimes must allow for some degree of pain in order to cut through the personal and social tensions that hold individuals back from growth. Ultimately, your actions will speak truths for a new generation of American citizens.

1

IN THE COMPANY OF RACISM

I have a dream that one day on the red hills of Georgia the sons of former slaves and the sons of former slave owners will be able to sit down together at the table of brotherhood.
— Dr. Martin Luther King, Jr.
Speech at Civil Rights March on Washington, D.C. [1963]

Thomas couldn't hide from his pain if he wanted to. He was nine years old. His family had just moved from a large city on the East coast to a suburb on the West coast. Like most newcomers, he found it difficult at first to make friends. Several other children lived on his block, but every time he tried to get close, they ran away. He didn't think much about it, however, especially after he met another nine-year-old boy named Stephen who lived four houses down and across the street. The two boys shared a common interest: baseball.

One Saturday afternoon, Thomas and Stephen went to the park. They had just watched a baseball game on television and were looking forward to playing in a make-believe World Series. Thomas pitched the ball to Stephen, who was crouched down as a catcher. As the ball came whizzing across home plate for a strike, Stephen gave the play-by-play: "Strike three and the batter's out." The boys laughed and took turns pitching and catching, hitting, and running.

Thomas hadn't noticed at the time, but he was the only African-American child in an otherwise

Playgrounds are where we form some of our first and most lasting impressions. Yet children don't emphasize differences in race or skin color until adults point them out, perpetuating the unfortunate and unnecessary cycle of racism.

all-white neighborhood. Even Stephen was white, but then, Thomas never had to worry about the color of his skin or that of someone else. It had never been an issue. "I just went to the park that day to play ball with my friend," he recalls. "It never crossed my mind that someone was looking at me and thinking that I was black and that I didn't belong in 'their' neighborhood."

As the two boys continued to play catch, a third boy came over to pick a fight with Thomas. "He started calling me 'nigger' this, and 'nigger' that. I was sort of getting upset, but deep down inside I felt really sad about it. I didn't know what to do."

A shouting match ensued and Thomas called the boy a dirty name. "I probably shouldn't have called him a name, but he was calling me names. Looking back, I know it wasn't nice." The boy hit Thomas in the face. Thomas struck back and they began to fight. "I was scared because my home was several blocks away. I didn't even know why we were fighting."

A crowd gathered and Thomas heard several other kids shout, "Kill the nigger! Kill the nigger!" He started to cry, and the other boys laughed at him. Several minutes passed before someone's father came over and separated them, scolding Thomas to quit causing trouble and to go back to his own neighborhood. Thomas looked over to his new friend Stephen for support, but the boy just turned his back on him. "That hurt more than the punches," he says. "I thought we were friends. Friends stick up for each other. I think he was scared, too."

Thomas walked home alone that day, and promised himself that he would never again play catch with another white boy. He has kept his promise for four years now. "I asked my mom later, 'Why do white people hate black people?' She just cried and said she didn't know. I still don't know, but I know enough not to hang around white people any more. I know I sound like a racist, but I've got experience with these matters. Black folks shouldn't mix with white folks. It's that simple."

WHAT IS RACISM?

Racism comes in many shapes and colors. African-Americans, Asians, Hispanics, Whites, American Indians, and members of other ethnic groups can carry racial prejudices with them. A racist can be young or old, rich or poor. He doesn't always carry a business card and he rarely shows his true character. He could be your teacher, your brother, or your best friend. He could come at you with a handshake or with a clenched fist. Some experts have even suggested there is some racism in all of us.

Even if you don't think of yourself as a bigot, you may still harbor strong negative feelings about another race. Have you ever been afraid of someone walking toward you because of the color of his skin? Have you listened to

Two youths in a New York City public school cafeteria: Have they formed quick, superficial, prejudiced judgments about each other, or are they just discussing one boy's preference for a certain pro hockey team?

someone tell a racial joke and laughed with everyone else at the punch line? Sooner or later, you will be confronted with an incident of racism. How you respond will always speak louder than your words.

We often say "racism" when what we really mean is prejudice or discrimination. Prejudice is a quick judgment of someone based on limited information, such as color. You may dislike an individual because of his race, even though you don't really know him. Discrimination occurs when you treat someone differently for reasons other than merit. A friend of yours may fail to get elected president of your student body because she's Hispanic. Is it possible to be prejudiced, but not discriminate? Experts say we can have strong negative feelings about a person, yet choose to keep them to ourselves. Making jokes about or even expressing dislike of a minority group is one thing; planning actions that amount to racism is quite another.

The most famous civil rights leader in America was Dr. Martin Luther King, Jr., who led millions of people in protest against racism in America.

Dr. Martin Luther King, Jr., referred to the difference between racism and prejudice when he said: "The law may not make a man love me, but it can restrain him from lynching me."

Most people think of race in terms of physical characteristics, such as skin color, hair texture, and facial features. In the past, a person of the "wrong" race often lived through difficult times. African-Americans, for example, were denied rights that others took for granted. Hispanics have been denied jobs because of their accents. Both practices are clearly racist. Although times are better now than when African-Americans were kept as slaves, many people believe we haven't gone far enough to secure freedom from discrimination for all people.

In his book *Majority-Minority Relations*, social scientist John E. Farley broadly defines racism as an attitude, belief, behavior, or institutional arrangement that tends to favor one race or ethnic group over another. He categorizes four kinds of racism:

- Attitudes or beliefs that favor one group over another (for example, a general dislike for a certain racial or ethnic group).
- Attitudes or beliefs that directly state that some races are superior to others (for example, Adolph Hitler's theory that white Germans were superior to all others).
- Behaviors that lead to unequal treatment on the basis of race (for example, taxi drivers who refuse to pick up minority customers).
- Behaviors that go beyond individual thoughts and actions, in which social institutions, such as family, church, school, and government create patterns of racial injustice and inequality, and reinforce racist ideas. (For example, the high cost of a college education can prevent lower-income students, who are often members of minority groups, from obtaining a college degree.)

CLASS AND ETHNIC RACISM

Racism is also a belief system of advantages based on class or ethnicity. Where we live and how much money our families make has a lot to do with the friends we keep. We tend to "stick to our own kind." Some people have little understanding of the ways in which their social and economic backgrounds have shaped their views of the world.

William lives in a nice neighborhood and wears nice clothes. His father is vice-president of a real estate company and can afford to buy him new tennis shoes and the latest clothing styles. At school, William has noticed that not everyone is as well-to-do as he. In fact, one of the students in his gym class wears shoes that are old, torn, and tattered. His clothes always look dirty and wrinkled. "He seems like a nice kid, but I don't want to be his friend because he seems so poor and pitiful," says William.

Racism can also be about a person's language, culture, sense of ancestry, and sometimes religion. Maria, age 15, feels as though she has been the target of racism because of her accent. She is from a small village in Mexico. Two years ago, she came to the United States to live with her aunt and cousin. Although her command of the English language was limited at the time, she took classes to improve her skills and was doing well.

Last summer, Maria went with her aunt and cousin to an amusement park in Southern California. One ride in particular fascinated her—the roller

Skin color or complexion is a notoriously inaccurate way to tell where someone comes from—or, for that matter, what sort of person they are. Can you tell whether these students are from Mexico, Armenia or Fiji? The answer is, it doesn't matter. They are sharing a school desk in Oakland, California, and their education is what matters.

coaster that splashed down on its final turn into a pool of water. "I couldn't wait to go on that ride," she remembers. "It was all I could think about. My cousin and I spent about 25 minutes in line waiting for our turn. It was a hot day and we were looking forward to getting wet. After a while, though, I noticed that some of the other children rode over and over again, but the sign said, 'One ride per ticket.' I asked the engineer why the other children were getting to ride the roller coaster more than one time, only I made a few mistakes with my words because I was nervous. He said it was because they could speak English and I couldn't."

Maria found her aunt and told her about the other children riding several times. Her aunt confronted the engineer and mentioned the sign that read one ride per ticket. Maria and her cousin were finally allowed to ride the roller coaster, but only one time. "Even as I was getting off, two white children in front of us asked the engineer if they could ride," Maria continues. "He looked at me as he told them 'yes,' and then he smiled." Nowadays, Maria keeps an eye out for this kind of behavior. "Up until then, I had been blind to how subtle racism can be in this country."

It's hard to get through a day without bumping into someone whose accent or style of dress are vastly different from your own. We are fast becoming a society in which members of diverse ethnic groups can develop their own special interests and still contribute to a common goal. Many of today's youths are part of a mixed-race generation where the color line is less obvious than it was 15 years ago.

Yvette is a good example. She has creamy skin, blue eyes, and reddish-blond hair. Her father is African-American and her mother is of European descent. Yvette's first cousin, Christopher, looks like a Pacific Islander, the child of a Japanese mother and an African-American father. "I define myself as African-American, but I'm also white," she says. "My cousin defines himself as African-American, but he's also part Japanese. Where do we fit in? Should we keep company with our black brothers and sisters, or our white and Japanese friends? Why should it even matter?"

Why does the color of a person's skin matter? Where does the African-American person with pale skin and straight hair fit in, or the white person with dark skin and full lips? Why should society have the right to define anyone, including you, simply because of how they look? Racism applies to more than just skin color. It is how students define themselves and others as part of a specific group. Almost everyone has a strong desire to belong to a group. You may want to align yourself with the "rich" kids, with the athletes and cheerleaders, or with other Jewish students. The issue is not so much where you belong, but how you treat others outside your group. Unless we begin to work on improving race relations, it will very likely turn into the most serious social problem of the 21st century.

WHY DO WE INVENT STEREOTYPES?

Experts who study social relationships call people who are targeted by racism the minority group. We tend to think of a majority as being the greatest in number, and the minority as being smaller. In most cases, that's true. Sometimes, however, majority and minority are not decided by quantity, but by power. Those with social power are the majority, while those without it are the minority.

The group that holds the power often places stereotypes on the group that doesn't. Stereotypes are oversimplified attitudes or judgments. They're like cartoons. They may be based on something real, but they are not an accurate view of any group of people, and are usually exaggerated. Stereotypes are almost always negative, and they strengthen the beliefs of the majority by implying that the minority is somehow inferior.

You can apply stereotypes to any group or class of people. Some people think of Jews as being overly interested in money or business. Others think all African-Americans are on welfare or that all American Indians live on reservations. Still others believe white people automatically carry prejudices against minorities, and that all Hispanics have large families. Of course, not a single one of these stereotypes is true.

Most of us tend to form stereotypes as a simple way of organizing information to make sense of our environment. When we meet people, we tend to categorize them based on their physical attributes or by the way they talk. Because race is one of the aspects of another person that we notice first, it's easier for us to categorize people that way. "Go talk to that black guy over there" or "Look at that Chinese woman" are examples of how we pigeonhole people. This kind of thinking can form a foundation for prejudices, especially if we want to satisfy basic needs for power and control for ourselves and others like us.

Stereotypes worsen when we take this misinformation and apply it across the board to every member of a particular group, and then form judgments. Every distorted piece of information is stored in our memory. Every time we read the newspaper, watch television, or listen in on a conversation about a class of people, we file the information in our memories for further reference. Even when personal experiences contradict our negative information, they continue to have a powerful, yet subtle, control over our thinking and actions. It is a lot easier to hang onto our simple, uncomplicated preconceptions than to fit new views into our tidy people file. Stereotypes save time. The following is an example of how stereotypes work.

Pamela, age 17, lives with her father, who is an engineer, and her mother, who works as an interior designer. Pamela is a cheerleader and a member of the swim team. She hopes to attend college next fall. About the only experience she has had with people of other races is with cheerleading. Yet, even this activity is somewhat segregated. "There's only one black girl on the cheerleading squad," says Pamela. "Yet blacks are such good dancers; they are the best dancers in the school. I don't understand why more of them don't try out for cheerleading.

"There isn't a lot of racial fighting, but there is tension on campus," she continues. "If I accidentally bump into a white girl, I don't get scared about it. But if I accidentally bump into a black girl or she bumps into me, I expect her to call me a name or to turn around and tell me to get out of her way or something. Black girls like to fight, and I know for a fact that they hate white girls. That's really generalizing, I know, but that's been my experience. My friends and I try to stay away from them."

Pamela doesn't think she's a prejudiced person, but she sits at lunch with only her white friends from her own neighborhood. "Everyone does," she says, by way of an explanation. "Hispanics sit with their friends, blacks sit in their area. It just happens that way."

Pamela's prejudices surface when she stereotypes certain people because of the color of their skin. She makes statements like "Blacks are such good dancers," "Black girls like to fight," and "I try to stay away from them." Pamela prefers not to be friends with African-Americans because she sees them as somehow different, maybe even inferior.

YEARS OF SCHOOLING

B reaking a stereotype is hard. Our perception of people is often based on years, and sometimes decades, of misinformation. Most of us tend to stereotype members of a particular group if we feel threatened by them or we don't understand or know them. We say they're not civilized because their culture is not the same as ours. We assume they're dangerous, or we think they're cunning and clannish. We call them lazy and half-witted because that's how they've been portrayed in the movies and on television. We either ignore them, try to take away their privileges, or try to protect and control them "for their own good," as well as for the good of society—that is, our society.

Stereotypes can also hurt members of the so-called privileged majority because they will miss out on some potentially rewarding human contacts. White students might remember the pain of having lost an important friendship because African-American friends were not allowed to visit their home. Even though some stereotypes may be considered positive (such as "Asian students

These students from various ethnic backgrounds have many things in common, including their interest in journalism and public relations. They don't stereotype each other according to appearances—they consider the individual and his or her talents.

are good in math"), they have negative effects in the long run, because they deny a person's individuality. However, you can make efforts to break a stereotype:

- Expose yourself to a broad range of experiences
- Build friendships with students of other races
- Take an interest in a culture different from your own
- Get to know people on a one-to-one basis

IS THERE SOME RACISM IN ALL OF US?

Some people think they're not prejudiced, but on a much deeper level, they probably have negative opinions about certain races and cultures. They tend to look at themselves as superior and at others as different and in need of improvement. They may even discriminate, act hostile, or talk down to people. In fact, most of the white population who say and probably believe they are not prejudiced may still show a modern, subtle form of bias. According to Professor John Dovidio, a research psychologist from Colgate University, 85 percent of white Americans harbor some form of subtle racism, while 15 percent are clearly racists. "I believe this subtle form of bias helps account for racism in our society," says Dovidio.

What exactly does Dovidio mean by subtle biases?

One of the ways we categorize people is by placing them into in-groups (us, we), and out-groups (them, they). According to Dovidio, we associate more positive qualities with "we" than with "they," and more negative qualities with "they" than with "we."

"That's not to say that the we/they distinction explains all racism or bias," says Dovidio. "Racism is much more complicated than that. But it should be emphasized again that our everyday actions and words may contribute to subtle forms of racial bias."

But how does this sort of thinking affect behavior? If you make decisions on a we/they basis, the outcome will be biased. Attitudes translate into the way people think, explains Dovidio, "and the way people think translates into the way people behave, sometimes in terms of discrimination."

As a nation made up of many different races and cultures, we Americans have been influenced by racial and cultural prejudice from the very beginning of our history. American Indians were forced to live on reservations by the first European settlers. African-Americans were imported as slaves. Hispanic immigrants driven by poverty moved to the Southwest, where they worked for extremely low wages as farm laborers.

Many of today's stereotypes are based on the same myths that surrounded the Irish, Italians, and other European immigrants of the previous century. The dangerous part of stereotyping is that we tend to see people in a distorted way. Those who fit into the stereotype just strengthen our belief that it is accurate. Pamela sees an African-American girl who is a good dancer and she thinks all African-Americans are good dancers. One expert who studies race relations says stereotypes are almost impossible to remove from our memories. "Once people get a stereotype in their heads to predict how someone else will act, they'll almost never let it go."

Racism may come in many shapes and colors, but the result is always the same—it destroys people's lives. Living in this country and not being exposed to some form of personal, cultural, or institutional racism is virtually impossible. Thomas was physically abused simply because of the color of his skin. Maria was passed over for a turn on the roller coaster because the engineer held prejudices. We are confronted with these issues on a daily basis and in ways of which we're not even aware.

Monique, age 17, recalls the time she was the only African-American teenager in a tennis tournament. On the day of the competition, she remembers feeling "nervous and intimidated." She had not been playing up to her potential for several weeks, and the other players were all exceptionally talented. Still, she

What our parents teach us at home has the greatest influence on our beliefs and values. Much of our attitudes toward people of other races—good and bad—comes from the example our parents set.

kept her composure and played her best. Even though she lost to a player who was definitely more skilled, she felt good about her performance. "I walked away with a feeling of accomplishment," she says. "I didn't win, but I gave her a good game."

After her match, Monique sat down in the audience to watch the other players. A white woman in the seat next to her leaned over and whispered in her ear. "Who do you think you are? You don't belong here. You should be playing basketball or something."

"I didn't know what to say to her," says Monique. "I wondered how many other people in the audience felt the same way. It made me self-conscious. I didn't play well my next match. I just felt really sad. Why do people have to be that way?"

RACISM OFTEN BEGINS AT HOME

A child may throw a rock at a playmate or call someone a name, and these actions may seem to exhibit hatred for another race, but usually it's a simple temper tantrum soon to be forgotten. As we get older, however, we begin to form real attitudes and feelings about people of different races. We may show our true colors by being cruel, unfair, or talking down to people. Later, the selection of our friends is no longer based on friendship, but on personal prejudices.

You acquire many of your attitudes from your parents, your brothers and sisters, your friends, and your teachers. Your father may have made a racial joke once and laughed about it with your mother. Maybe your grandfather smiled when you used a nasty expression to describe another race. Many textbooks still only give credit to European-Americans for having "done it all" in this country, instead of citing the contributions of people of color. Although none of these examples may involve conscious effort to turn you into a racist, prejudices may still be the result, even if unintentional.

Jennifer's father is a member of a white supremacy group. She was raised to believe that African-Americans are inferior to whites, and that all Jewish people are evil. She's a 16-year-old girl who has been taught to hate from an early age. Although she attends a public school of mixed races, she sticks only to her white friends. "I believe blacks and Jews are the devil's sons and daughters," she says. "I hate what they stand for."

Kelly, on the other hand, remembers her first encounter with an Hispanic man. She was seven years old and visiting her grandparents in a part of Ohio where there were few non-white people. One afternoon, a man with brown skin and dirty clothes approached her in the park. Her father had always said: "Mexicans are dirty, lazy, and uncivilized," Kelly recalls. "This was the first Mexican who ever approached me. I kept hearing my father's voice telling me, 'Stay away from the Mexicans.'" When the Hispanic man started talking to her in Spanish, she became frightened and ran home.

Kelly tried to explain to her grandfather what had happened. He asked her if she had even seen up close one of the laborers who worked the fields in the next county. She said she had not. Her grandfather then tried to explain to her how there are people in this world who speak different languages and pray to different gods. Kelly listened to her grandfather's words, but could only hear her father's voice telling her to "stay away." Looking back on that incident, she knows now her grandfather was a wise man, but his wisdom never made an impact on her opinion of Hispanic men. Even today, she feels the same fear come over her when she sees an Hispanic man. "I try to hide or ignore my prejudices, but it's always there. I know it's wrong, but I can't help the way I feel."

Racism often springs from people's sense that they are being threatened by forces they don't completely understand and can't control. Contrary to what some people believe, there is nothing natural about racism. Although most of our racial attitudes are often a reflection of the environment in which we are raised, we can acquire prejudices in other ways. Maybe we had a personal experience with a person of another race that turned out badly. Maybe society has influenced our thinking. Have you ever heard of or belonged to a private social club or organization that excludes certain races? Movie and television studios often assume that stories about a certain class of people are more interesting or entertaining than others, and therefore more profitable to make. Movies with different perspectives often don't even get made.

Racism exists because of the acts of individuals who either make and carry out discriminatory practices or who allow them to continue without protesting. Sometimes, cultural misunderstandings at school or in society create intense prejudice. Sometimes competition for jobs, government benefits, or admission to schools can cause friction. These influences are extremely dangerous because they affect so many people.

For example, if you are living in a neighborhood that is favored by banks and insurance companies, you are receiving advantages that people in other neighborhoods don't enjoy, even though you haven't chosen to receive the advantages and might even choose to give them up—if you had a choice.

Because of the prejudice and racism inherent in our environments when we were children, we cannot be blamed for learning what we were taught (intentionally or unintentionally). Yet as we get older, we have a responsibility to try to identify and interrupt the cycle, and improve our attitudes and behaviors toward every man, woman, and child, regardless of their skin color, economic status, and cultural background.

A "WHITE" VIEW ON RACISM

Is racism something we learned as a child or are we born with it? Former school teacher Jane Elliott has her own theory. "Racism is not part of human nature," she says. "You are born into a racist society. You are not born to be a racist. Racism is a learned response and, like anything else, if you can learn it, you can unlearn it."

Elliott is the former elementary school teacher who is best known for her blue-eyed, brown-eyed experiments. The day after Dr. Martin Luther King, Jr. was assassinated, Elliott had to figure out a way of explaining the concept of racism to her third graders in an all-white community of Iowa. "The only thing I could think of was to allow them to walk in the shoes of a child of color."

To that end, students with blue eyes were told they were better than those with brown eyes. They were told they were smarter and were given special class privileges for the day. Those with the wrong color eyes were placed in the same position society places minority groups. "They were treated the way people of color are treated in this country," explains Elliott, "and they reacted exactly the way people of color react in this country—with anger.

"When I told my brown-eyed students that they weren't as smart, they immediately became less able to perform academically," she continues. "The blue-eyed students immediately practiced the racism they had learned in society. They became arrogant, belligerent, and smug, all the signs we typically associate with racist people. These third graders knew how racism works, although they couldn't have told you how it works."

When Elliott reversed the groups—told the brown eyes they were better than the blue eyes—the results changed accordingly.

Elliott believes these students and other students across the country learn this type of behavior by copying the adults in their environment, from television, from movies, and from the curriculum in their schools. She denounces the myth of a colorblind society. "When you hear somebody say that, 'I don't see people as black or brown or red or yellow, I just see people,' you know you're listening to a racist because what he's really saying is, 'There's something wrong with this person's color, so we just will pretend he isn't this color.'"

The educational system also contributes to racism by not accurately portraying the contributions of African-Americans and other people of color, Elliott adds. "Students must realize the contributions that have been made to society, to civilization by people of color. Most of us are not aware of these things because we live in a racist society and because we're educated in a racist school system that only teaches us about white contributions."

Over the years, Elliott has conducted the same blue-eyed, brown-eyed experiment with college students, politicians, military officers, and corporate executives. The results were always the same: The privileged groups practiced the equivalent of racism, while the underprivileged groups became angry.

To get beyond the hate and anger, Elliott believes you must first quit denying that racism exists. "If you allow others to convince you that racism is just part of human nature, you will never change," she adds. "It's not human nature to hate someone because of their skin color. We underestimate the intelligence of students by thinking they can't handle the truth, but they can. And the truth is racism is a learned response."

2

ON THE FRONT LINES

No one can make you feel inferior without your consent.
— Eleanor Roosevelt, *This is My Story* [1937]

Sharona was a 10th grader when she first took a stand against racism. It happened two years ago in Chicago, where she spent her summer visiting with relatives, who live in an all-white neighborhood. Her family is from India. They came to the United States when she was a child, and she considers herself an American.

As she stood in line waiting to pay for an ice cream, a white woman carrying several items was behind her. A white cashier was behind the counter. "She asked me to get in the back of the line so that the woman with a lot of groceries could get in front of me," Sharona recalls. "I didn't know what to do at first, but I thought about it and I started to get mad. So I said, 'No, I was here first.'"

The woman behind the counter started to scream at Sharona. "Get out of the way, you foreigner!" she said, adding other obscenities. Sharona stood her ground. Her voice trembled as she yelled back at the woman. "No! I was here first and I have only ice cream to buy!" The manager of the store came over and asked Sharona to leave. "I explained to him what had happened," she says. "He looked at me and then at the woman behind the counter, and said: 'If she was here first, she should go first. Let her pay for her ice cream.' I could tell the woman behind the counter was mad, but she had no

To begin conquering racism, all of us must take a stand and announce to others that treating people differently because of their race is unacceptable.

Bothered by racial conflicts at school? Form a campus group to help deal with the problem and show fellow students methods they can use to get along.

choice. I paid for my ice cream, then walked over to the manager and thanked him for his help. He smiled at me and said he was sorry for what the woman behind the counter called me, and that he would have a talk with her about it later. I walked away feeling good about myself and about the human race in general."

A senior who attends Sharona's high school talks about the time she was the target of racism. As a child, Masako had practically no friends among the other Japanese students in her class. Her family lived in a mostly white neighborhood and most of her playmates in school and at church were white children. When her family moved to a new city, her life changed in ways she could never imagine.

Masako began to notice that she was not readily accepted by the white students at her new school, even though she was very nice and above average in intelligence. She tried to make friends with the Japanese students, but she found that she was not made to feel entirely at home there, either. She became lonely and depressed.

"I didn't make a point of having only white friends in my old neighborhood," she explains. "It just worked out that way. But when we moved to Chicago, I just wanted a friend, period. I didn't care what color or race she turned out to be. The white students saw me as Japanese, however, and the Japanese students saw me as trying to act white. I was caught in the middle."

She went to her counselor and explained her problem. They talked it over and decided there might be other students who were feeling the same sort of isolation and loneliness that Masako was feeling. So they formed an after-school club that welcomed students of all races who were interested in learning more about each other. By the end of the semester, Masako had made friends from all walks of life. "I didn't realize how many other students were just as confused as I was about race relations," she says. "I'm just glad we were able to share our experiences. It made me feel a lot better."

Why is it that, despite the civil rights movement and other positive social changes over the years, we still are confronted with racism on a daily basis? Racism can make you angry or sad. Why do we tend to distinguish people by their race, class, or culture, and not by their character?

Almost everyone has a basic need to identify with a specific race. It helps to define yourself and others. In each case, a positive sense of who you are as a member of a group is assumed to be important for psychological health. This process can hinder friendships among people of different races when one group assumes superiority over the other, however.

CONFRONTING RACISM

Greg is a football player on his high school team. Jesse enjoys tennis and is a band member. For several months, Greg has been taunting Jesse, who is Hispanic. At first, it was only a comment or two. Greg would call Jesse names and make racial jokes about his family. The other boys would laugh. Jesse let it go because he thought it would eventually blow over, but it didn't.

Greg's attitude toward Jesse got worse. He started pushing Jesse around and taking his tennis racket. One day, Jesse had had enough. He got mad and tried to punch Greg, only he missed. Greg, who was a lot stronger than Jesse, gave him a black eye and bloody nose. "I couldn't take it anymore," says Jesse. "I had no other choice but to fight him."

Victor is also Hispanic. He looks back on his childhood with fond memories. Last year, he made the freshman basketball team at school. He learned the sport playing with his cousins in Mexico. He was a good point guard, and great free-throw shooter. He made a lot of friends in a short period of time. But when the team went on road trips, Victor always felt a little out of place. His teammates, who were mostly white, would make cracks on the bus about Hispanics.

On one particular road trip, Victor's teammates were especially cruel. As they passed a group of Hispanics, they shouted out words like "greaser" and "dirty Mexican." During one particularly offensive volley, Victor himself made an off-color joke about Hispanics. His teammates approved. One guy sitting behind him slapped Victor on the back, as if he had just scored two points. "It wasn't until several weeks later that I realized how terrible I felt making rude comments about my own heritage," says Victor. "It made me hate myself so much that I quit the team."

If you feel as though you're being discriminated against, or if someone close to you is being threatened with violence because of the color of his or her skin, don't hesitate to take action. You're not alone. Your community has organizations and people who will help you.

Ask yourself why someone is harassing you or your friends. Maybe he or she was raised in a family that encouraged hate. Maybe he or she is feeling insecure and vulnerable, and is blaming you. These feelings only make matters more difficult. Racists have a psychological need to feel superior to others. Try not to get upset. Don't lose your own self-esteem, even though you or your friends are being attacked because of your ethnicity.

Find personal ways of dealing with racism. Stop listening to racist jokes. Don't tolerate racist discussions at the dining table or anywhere else. If necessary, confront racists about their attitudes, but do it without making them feel guilty. Try to decrease their defensiveness by keeping the conversation light and friendly. Any other way is counterproductive. Above all else, continue to educate yourself and be committed to doing the right thing.

ONE TEACHER'S APPROACH

We are on the front lines of racism every day. We can choose to ignore the problem, which many people do, or we can meet it head-on. Sharona decided to confront her fears by standing up to the white woman behind the counter. Masako confided in an adult, her school counselor, and designed a program to bring together people with different backgrounds. Both approaches worked.

Have you ever taken a stand against racism? When was the last time you befriended a person of a different race? Do you have the courage and strength to form a support group in your school? Last year, students at Kennedy Middle School in Springfield, Massachusetts, found racial tensions growing between a group of African-American students and a group of Puerto Rican students. A fight eventually broke out between two eighth-graders. "They became angry and started to call each other names. That's where racism came into play," says Jeralyn Grandison, a teacher at Kennedy Middle School.

"The black girls are always making up things to fight about," says one of the Puerto Rican girls. "So I called her a nigger. I didn't realize then how much that hurt."

Fortunately, two of the girls went to the principal's office and asked for help before things got out of hand. "We couldn't come up with a solution, but I told them to hold off and wait to see if we couldn't come up with a better way," says Grandison. As a result of the fight between the Puerto Rican students and the African-American students, Grandison designed a program at Kennedy Middle School that helps dispel myths and stereotypes.

They started holding meetings after school to deal one-on-one with the issue of racism. Grandison recommended the students first obtain a mediator—someone who could be fair, yet firm. She then suggested they try role-playing because "it helps reenact an argument, which can lead to a better solution." Finally, Grandison had them write down their feelings because it sometimes helps to release the anger. "If we can just get beyond the anger and name calling, we can get to the root of the problem," explains Grandison. "And that's when the healing starts."

Grandison feels students of different races don't spend enough time learning about each other. "They wanted to get along, so I told them to stop dwelling on the differences and find out what they have in common." Unfortunately, it's not always that easy. What one teenager may think of as reasonable behavior may seem racist to another teenager. Sometimes it's just about ethnic pride, as was the case between the African-American and Puerto Rican students at Kennedy Middle School. Too much emphasis on ethnic pride can actually worsen race relations and lead to conflict.

Experts say it is the degree to which students differ from one another that causes conflict. This could mean the degree of "whiteness," the degree to which they differ in religion, language, or values, or the degree to which they have been accepted by their peers. It's not unusual to start feeling hostile toward someone who doesn't accept you or respect you, whether they say so or not.

For many of today's teenagers, pride in one's heritage is a quick and convenient way of dealing with the harsh realities of everyday living. Many parents have been laid off from work, or struggle to carve out a decent life while

Many schools hold special workshops, such as this one featuring teenagers from the Greater Boston Regional Youth Council, to promote cross-cultural awareness.

working for meager salaries. Teenagers are caught in the middle. Should they stay in school and go to college, or should they drop out and find a job to help out at home? Many struggle with such decisions. They need something to hang on to that will give them pride and self-respect, so they turn to their peers. One common tactic is to form gangs and fight over turf with other groups.

"We're facing extinction," says the 17-year-old member of a Skinhead gang, a young, mostly white-male version of the American Nazi Party. "I'm like a wolf when its children are threatened. I will do anything to ensure the survival of my children. In 10 years, I'll either be dead, incarcerated by the government, or living in an all-white country.

"I'm so tired of everything being turned into a racial issue," he continues. "I'm tired of people looking at my skin and not only judging me, but thinking I owe them something. What's wrong with looking and acting white? I'm proud of who I am."

Says an African-American teenager: "In my opinion, blacks excel in all fields, despite the cards we've been dealt. We're good in sports, in architecture, and we do well in all types of business. I really believe that as a people, we are doing all right on our own. We owe it to ourselves to keep doing what we're doing better and better and to keep doing it right. We owe it to ourselves not to let other people get in our way. Our people need to keep rising to higher and higher levels of achievement in whatever we choose to do. I don't think that anybody owes us anything. I believe that we owe it to ourselves to do the best we can at all times."

CAUGHT IN THE MIDDLE

Mostafa was 16 years old when Operation Desert Storm was mounted against Iraq, primarily by the U.S. military, again focusing the attention of Americans everywhere on Arabs and Islam, the religious faith of Muslims.

Mostafa was on his high school wrestling team at the time. He lived with his mother in a small house behind the school he attended in the Midwest. Every morning before sunrise, he would jog through the wheat fields between his house and the school to make it early to wrestling practice. He felt it built stamina and made him tougher as a competitor.

During the time of Operation Desert Storm, Mostafa was accused by a number of students of being in support of Iraq, even though he was Iranian by ancestry. "The other kids didn't realize that Iran was once in a war with Iraq, that we were enemies, too," says Mostafa. "I tried to explain it to them, but they didn't want to listen. They were too interested in wanting to appear patriotic."

During the Gulf War, there were many reported incidents of Arab-Americans being beaten or harassed—even those who were not even of Iraqi descent. Just "looking" Arabic was enough. Mostafa ended up being one of them. It happened when he was jogging through the wheat fields early one morning. He was confronted by a group of teenage boys he thought he recognized from

People with racist attitudes might not bother to discover that this woman and her child are refugees from Afghanistan. Sadly, too many of us think we know who people are by their looks, and what "they" represent, and we are often wrong.

a cross-town high school, although he couldn't be certain when he was asked by police to give a report. The boys accused him of being a citizen of Iraq and of failing to support the American troops. The larger of the boys punched Mostafa in the nose, knocking him to the ground. The other three then started kicking him. "I kept telling them that I was Iranian, but they couldn't understand the difference. They saw what they wanted to see—a Middle Eastern enemy of the United States."

Americans sometimes exhibit a sense of nationalism when our world affairs are not in order. Citizens of other nations do the same thing. Nationalism is loyalty and devotion to one nation above all others. As a country, we sometimes use our loyalties to justify racism. In recent years, this devotion has led to a new type of prejudice against Arab-Americans who have been blamed for everything from high oil prices to Iran's taking of American hostages back in the late 1970s.

The bombing of the World Trade Center in New York on February 26, 1993, only made matters worse. Six people were killed and more than 1,000 injured by a bomb believed to have been planted by a group of terrorists from the Arab community.

The reason for our stereotypes toward Arabs—or for any other minority group—is because of a perceived or actual threat against our physical, social, or economic health. We, in turn, try to restrict their opportunities so we can reduce the imaginary threat, and then develop more negative stereotypes to justify our discriminatory ways. It's a vicious cycle. Homeowners may fear that the presence of a new ethnic group will make property values go down. People who are out of work may blame immigrants because jobs are hard to find. When the crime rate soars, many people direct their anger at minorities, blaming them for the problem.

During Operation Desert Storm, one study indicated that those Americans who felt Arab-Americans were an economic threat were more prejudiced than others. Arab-Americans were stereotyped as a clan of people who are backward and uncivilized, ruthless and barbaric, who either strongly supported terrorists or were terrorists themselves.

During World War II, Japanese-Americans faced a similar type of discrimination. Because America was at war with Japan, many people feared Japanese descendants who lived in this country. Once again, this fear was based more on racism than on anything else. America, however, was also at war with Germany and Italy, yet there was less fear of German-Americans and Italian-Americans. People's myths and stereotypes about "evil Asians" led to laws that allowed property to be confiscated and Japanese-Americans to be imprisoned in detention camps. Ironically, the sons of these same Americans were often in the U.S. armed services, fighting for the country that was imprisoning their families simply on the basis of their racial ancestry.

Arab-Americans number approximately 2.5 million, representing about one percent of the U.S. population. They come from many different cultures, countries, and economic situations, much like Hispanics and Asians. Sometimes, however, those whose prejudices keep them from paying attention to these important differences lump Arab-Americans—and other minorities—together into a single group.

Are there any Arab-American students on your campus? How were they treated during the war with Iraq? Mostafa felt as though he were attacked because the teenage boys thought of themselves as being part of a superior group. One of the worst effects of prejudice and nationalism is the way that it wipes out individual and cultural differences, as well as hurting the victim in emotional and even physical ways.

FINANCIAL RACIAL DISCRIMINATION

Racial discrimination in the United States continues to affect the chances of African-Americans to rise to better-paid positions. In 1989, for example, black men with one to three years of college were paid $825 for each $1,000 of income of their white counterparts.

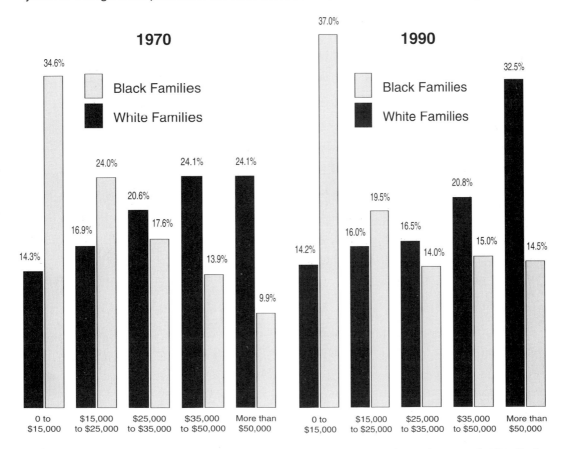

Source: Andrew Hacker. Two Nations: Black and White, Separate, Hostile, Unequal. *New York, NY: Charles Schribner's Sons, 1992.*

THE PROBLEM IS SKIN-DEEP

S ylvia grew up in Oakland, California. She seldom ventured outside her own predominantly African-American neighborhood, so she never came across prejudice in public places. When she got older and started visiting restaurants in other cities, her experiences were different. On occasion, she became offended by shoddy treatment or what struck her as odd requirements for service. At first, she didn't think much about it. "I started noticing a pattern, and it bothered me," she says.

One night, she and her girlfriend stopped for something to eat at a first-class restaurant in another city. "My girlfriend stood in line while I parked the car. When I came back, she was at the beginning of line and I thought, 'Great!'"

Whites and blacks couldn't sit together at this North Carolina lunch counter in the past. These Boston youths are touring famous sites in the Civil Rights movement as part of their high school education.

Then a white man came up to the maitre d' and asked, "How long is the wait?" The hostess approached with two menus to seat Sylvia and her friend, but the maitre d' stepped forward and told her to seat this white man first.

"I've never given anyone trouble," says Sylvia, "but that didn't sit well with me. I confronted the maitre d' and he just looked at me as if I were crazy. It's happened again. Sometimes, they go out of their way to make me feel uncomfortable. They look at me as if I'm an animal. I try to keep my composure, but sometimes I just get fed up with having to fight it."

Minorities can confront racism almost anywhere in society. Thirty years ago, civil rights leaders organized sit-ins at lunch counters that refused to serve people who were African-American. Today, the problem persists as a new generation of African-Americans meets bias in restaurants and public places. In Milwaukee, a group of African-American college students stopped for snacks at a chain restaurant that advertised that it was open 24 hours a day. The students could see clearly through the windows that customers were eating, but the manager told them, "We're not serving, we're closed." Similar scenes have occurred in restaurants across the country—in California, Kentucky, South Carolina, and Texas. A federal judge approved a settlement requiring the restaurant chain in Milwaukee to pay $185,000 to make up for the December, 1991, incident.

Today, some restaurants still try to impose special cover charges on minorities. Others refuse to serve the advertised specials to minorities. Still others force minorities to wait in line while whites are ushered ahead. In several court cases, employees have said they were encouraged by managers to limit the number of African-Americans in their restaurants. "I see more direct evidence of discrimination now than in the late '70s," says one civil rights attorney.

Several possible explanations exist for the continued bias in this country:

(1) Restaurant management has associated the color of a person's skin with crime and gangs
(2) Fewer affirmative action programs are in the workplace
(3) A larger African-American middle class is appearing where once only whites were seen, causing managers to confront their own prejudices.

University of Florida sociologist Joseph Feagin, who is white, interviewed 350 middle-class African-Americans in 18 cities. "I didn't even ask an explicit question about public accommodations," he says. "I thought we had at least made progress there. But people started volunteering stories." When he finished his survey, Feagin was astonished to discover that 90 percent of his subjects were certain they had been victims of racism in restaurants, as well as in hotels, motels, and stores.

YOUR ATTITUDES ON RACISM

What you think and believe about current racial tensions can predict how you will treat people who are different from you. Our attitudes toward one another can mean the difference between making a friend or facing an enemy.

A study by the Reebok Foundation and Northeastern University confirmed that most high school students recognize the existence of discrimination, and that 30 percent of them are fully prepared to openly join in racial or religious incidents when they erupt. More than 90 percent of the students surveyed, however, agreed that if racial prejudice is to end in this country, all people must practice what they preach when they say that everyone should be treated alike, regardless of race, creed, or color.

The Reebok survey also showed that most African-Americans believe race conditions in society have worsened, while whites believe they have improved. African-Americans also feel that they are worse off in areas of education, housing, and justice, while whites believe just the opposite.

This national survey of a cross-section of 1,865 high school students also found that nearly half of them have joined in a racial or religious attack against peers, or believed the victims got what they deserved. "Our children have learned how to hate," says Richard Lapchick, at Northwestern University in Boston.

Several other highlights from the Reebok survey are:

- A majority of high school students have seen or heard about racial confrontations with overtones of violence, with African-American students more likely to have seen them.

- Thirty percent of high school students are prepared to intervene to stop or condemn a racial incident. Hispanic-Americans are more likely to get involved than white or African-American students.

- One in four students report that they have been the target of an incident of racial or religious bias. The most likely to have been targeted are African-Americans (46 percent), followed by Hispanics (22 percent).

- Four in 10 students report that when they see someone from another race or religion doing something they do not like, they are tempted to ask, "What else can you expect from those types of people?"

- While slightly more than half of the students would tell their parents about a racial incident that they saw, only one in four would tell a teacher or other school authority.

- Athletics in school tend to help reduce racial tensions because athletes become friends with someone of another race or religion.

- Roughly 75 percent of the students surveyed believe everyone has a right to "live in an environment free of violence." This opinion was held equally among different races and cultures.

- Sixty percent of students are interested in learning more about the culture and history of their own and other racial groups.

According to Louis Harris, the pollster who conducted the Reebok survey, "America faces a critical situation. Our findings show that racial and religious harassment and violence are now commonplace among our young people rather than the exception. Far from being concentrated in any one area, confrontations occur in every region of the country and in all types of communities."

The survey further made it clear that most students recognize the existence of discrimination but do not act on it, probably as a result of their reluctance to tell teachers or other school authorities when such incidents occur.

"This indicates that the students have little faith in the authorities' ability to help in either quelling the outbreaks or in taking the lead in getting at the root causes for the trouble," the study concludes. Yet students also said that they wanted to get involved in working in programs to make America more of a land of opportunity for everyone regardless of racial or ethnic background. The Reebok study concludes: "A way must be found to help students get involved in the type of activities that will help them realize their desire to make things better for everyone."

Source: Northeastern University's Center for the Study of Sport in Society.

3

CROSSING THE COLOR BARRIER

*The silent hatred that we all carry needs to be stripped. You
need to grow up. I'm not asking you to come across the street
and kiss me, I'm asking you to leave me alone.*
— Comedian Bill Cosby
speaking at a conference on Racism,
University of Massachusetts [September 1993]

After two years of dating, Reggie and Tseng
were convinced they would eventually get
married. It had been a tough road to travel, but they
seemed to be making it. He was an African-
American who played football and had ambitions of
becoming an architect. She was a Chinese-American
student who wanted to be a teacher. Their differences kept them strong. He was strong and outgoing.
She was gentle and reflective. As easy as they made
it look, they faced hurtful stereotypes—and not just
from their friends, either.

They first fell in love when she bumped into
him in the hall at school. They kept their relationship
a secret for almost six months. Tseng says she was
worried about her family's reaction. Tseng's mother
discovered the truth by accident when she found a
picture of them together at a high school dance. "I
didn't know what to say to my mother," recalls
Tseng. "Finally, I just admitted it."

Tseng's worst fears were confirmed. Her decision to date a non-Chinese person was unacceptable
to her parents. He was Western. She was Eastern.
How could they adjust to each other, her parents
wanted to know? Her parents asked her not to date
Reggie. When she said she could not obey, they were

*Interracial dating and marriage are still not common in our
society, because many people still object to races "mixing."*

deeply hurt. Explains Reggie: "Dating someone from another race or culture takes a lot of energy, let alone educating parents who are fighting their own biases and prejudices."

"Before I met Reggie, I never had extensive contact with African-Americans," says Tseng's mother, adding that her lack of exposure made it easy for her to believe negative generalizations about African-American people. "I believed all black people were on welfare, and that they commit crimes—that type of thing. Nobody I knew had ever challenged these things."

Dating is difficult enough between people of similar backgrounds. Interracial dating, on the other hand, is another area where racism can come into play in a teenager's life. If your parents don't object, your friends do. Friends suggested to Reggie, for instance, that he was abandoning his African-American heritage, that his relationship with Tseng indicated he had a problem with his own ethnicity.

Once, a classmate—who, like Tseng, had immigrated to America from China—told her that he didn't like African-American people. They were not honest, he said, and didn't work hard. "Sometimes I have to tell people, not in a hostile way, that my boyfriend is black. So if they have anything negative to say or stereotypical jokes, they can save them for other people."

Today, family and friends on both sides say their opposition was grounded in love. "People do judge you based on the color of your skin," says Reggie, noting the clashes between Koreans and blacks during the Los Angeles riots in 1992. "How do you rise above the bigotry?"

Reggie and Tseng are doing their best to set an example. Recently, someone asked Reggie, "When you look at your girlfriend, don't you think about the fact that she's Chinese?" He recalls his answer: "No, I think, 'She's my girlfriend.'"

Reggie and Tseng are just one of a growing number of teenagers for whom battling racism is a family affair. In 1991, roughly 1.9 percent of marriages consisted of interracial couples. Of those, about a quarter were unions of African-Americans and whites.

The decision to marry or not to marry a person of another race is an individual choice. The real problem, however, comes from family, friends, and the stares of strangers who oppose interracial couples. A white woman who was married to an African-American man received this advice once from a colleague: "If you want to get ahead, don't display a family portrait on your desk." No one has ever come right out and told Tseng that she's dating a lazy liar. Several people who don't know her boyfriend, however, who have never even seen him, have said as much. Some have even expected her to agree.

Each successful multiethnic relationship offers a little bit of living proof that when it comes to race, differences need not always divide.

DISCOVERING YOUR ROOTS

These days, with more and more teenagers coming from multi-racial backgrounds, there's a growing interest in discovering our roots—that is, our ethnic heritage, which is not always visible to the naked eye.

Linda, a senior in high school, has a father who is Hispanic, African-American, and American Indian, and a mother who is African-American. For many years, she did not use the Spanish pronunciation of their last name. "For a long time, when people asked what I was I would say, 'Black, period.' Eventually I realized that not acknowledging the other things in me would almost be a backlash against those parts, and I'm not ashamed of them either. Now when people ask, I tell them I'm African-American, Hispanic, and American Indian. The deepest part of me identifies with being black, but by pronouncing our surname the Spanish way, my sister and I can pay homage to those ancestors, too."

At some time in our lives all of us must understand and be proud of our heritage, our roots. This child from Pryor, Montana honors her Crow Indian ancestry during "American Indian Day" at school.

Whitney, who is part African-American and part Vietnamese, has painful memories of being tormented by African-American peers who were uncomfortable with how different she looked. Once, while walking down a street with several of her junior high school classmates, she had her ponytail chopped off by a group of African-American girls who took offense at the swing of her long, straight hair. "I can't help the way I look," she says. "Why should I be punished because my parents come from different ethnic backgrounds?"

ETHNIC PRIDE

Where does this concept of ethnic pride come from? Historically, the conditions under which we come into contact with each other set the pace for our future relations. It started with the first European explorers who came to this land and destroyed the languages, religions, and traditions of several million

American Indians. Later, it was the harsh relationship between European-Americans and African-Americans that laid the foundation for the growth of ethnic pride.

In Colonial America and until the Civil War, slaves were considered less than human, capable of performing only certain kinds of work. They were legally defined as property. They did not have the freedom to choose a husband or wife,

CHANGING ATTITUDES?

Have attitudes changed? Over the years, whites have slowly described African-Americans in less negative terms. According to one nationwide poll, this change demonstrates that, at least in what they say, white Americans are gradually becoming less prejudiced. The following statements and questions were asked of white Americans in 1975-76 and again in 1985.

How strongly would you object if a member of your family wanted to bring an African-American friend home for dinner?		Would Object	Would Not Object
	1975-76	28%	72%
	1985	16%	84%

White people have a right to keep African-Americans out of their neighborhoods if they want to, and African-Americans should respect that right.		Agree	Disagree
	1975-76	39%	61%
	1985	25%	75%

If your party nominated an African-American for president, would you vote for him if he were qualified for the job?		Yes	No
	1975-76	82%	18%
	1985	85%	15%

Source: Davis, James, Allan and Smith, Tom W., General Social Surveys, 1972-1987 cumulative code book. Chicago: National Opinion Research Center 1987.

These youths are putting on a workshop for other youngsters on how to express themselves without resorting to anger or stereotypes that poison debate and cause friction between ethnic groups.

to raise their own children, or to preserve their families in any way. They were cut off from their religions, their languages, and their cultures, and submerged in a culture based on the idea that they were possessions of white people.

Hispanic-Americans, on the other hand, came to the U.S. at a time when laws severely restricted immigration. If they were here illegally, they were limited in the types of jobs they could get because they had to hide their identities from the authorities to avoid being deported. Jewish-Americans faced anti-Semitism from the moment they first set foot in America. Many Asians have done well economically, which has prompted hostility from other minorities.

Improving race relations is no longer just a matter of bringing people together. Manning Marable, director of the Institute for Research in African-American Studies at Columbia University, believes that before significant change can occur, we must all become more aware of how we benefit from a system of power and authority that privileges some people, but not others. "The first step is recognition," he says.

MAKING THE CONNECTION

Getting along with people who are different from us is never easy. It takes a commitment to change your own views and attitudes. Here is a list of attitudes that can block positive relations.

- *A person's skin color is unimportant*—Most students like to take pride in who they are and where they come from. Purposely ignoring a person's skin color is like saying, "Your heritage is not important to me."
- *Open recognition of color may embarrass people*—It's okay to acknowledge your differences, just as long as you don't assume you're any better or worse for it. Open recognition of color may oftentimes lead to open communication.
- *I'm free of racism*—Experts believe there is some racism in all of us. Admitting you have negative feelings about another race is one of the first steps toward unlearning prejudices and racisms.

Now let's look at a list of attitudes that can encourage positive relations:

- *People count as individuals*—The sooner we can learn to accept people for who they are, the sooner we can learn to get along. It's not the color of their skin that matters, but the strength of their character.
- *Everyone, regardless of race, has feelings and aspirations*—Students who are different from you still share the same emotions. They laugh, they cry, and they hurt when someone judges them based on the color of their skin.
- *I may be part of the problem*—Take a long, hard look at your own attitudes and beliefs about other races. Recognizing your own prejudices helps you to better deal with them.

You must be willing to express your feelings openly and honestly, and to expose yourself to other races and cultures. If you can't do that, you'll never overcome your fears. Try helping others to understand their own feelings. Take risks by being the first to confront racism. Above all, assume responsibility for your own motives. Learn to recognize your own attitudes on racism.

TEARING DOWN THE WALLS

Most people do not accept racism as part of their own perspective. They see it as someone else's problem. Any one of us might be a racist in the sense that we see and respond to people who are different, and we have certain feelings and/or stereotypes about them that we do not have about people of our own race. Here are just a few ways of getting beyond the racism barrier:

- Move beyond your guilt and acknowledge your own and society's racism. Leave the past behind you and commit yourself to a better future.
- Accept the notion that everyone is entitled to his or her own opinions. You don't have to be pals with everyone, and you don't have to be used by anyone.
- Appreciate each other's differences, but do not feel compelled to imitate them or demand that they be like you.

WATCH WHAT YOU SAY

Have you ever made a racial slur by accident, and then tried to get out of it by saying something like, "But some of my best friends are black," or used the term "them" or "those people" in reference to a particular ethnic group? While these terms may seem inoffensive, they tend to take away individuality.

A California state legislator distributed a handout with a poem that described undocumented workers as, "baby-breeding free-loaders bent on supplanting the white race." Naturally, he was criticized by outraged Hispanic legislators and others. The assemblyman later apologized, telling a reporter that he thought the poem was clever and funny. "I am not a racist by any stretch of the imagination," he insisted. "I didn't mean to offend anyone."

Another legislator from California used the anti-Semitic phrase "Jew down" in a televised hearing to explain how a negotiator might gain financial advantage over another.

The people who make these remarks deny they are racists. Certainly, they are not spouting the kind of hatred associated with the Ku Klux Klan or the Aryan Nation. How is it, then, that people who pride themselves on being enlightened and sensitive can casually make remarks that others find offensive?

Subconsciously, we all do it. Some of us use negative terms for African-Americans and Hispanics, although we don't really consider them offensive. Others use negative terms for whites and Asians. We tend to resist acknowledging that our comments may be offensive to others.

Language reflects the biases and values of a culture, says linguist Selase Williams, chairman of the Pan-African studies department at California State University, Northridge. In this country, however, offensive language has been applied mostly to people of color. We "blacklist" people, we talk about the "black sheep" of the family. There are others. Many people use these terms without reservation. "People don't realize the impact this has," says Williams.

English is full of expressions that hurt members of other racial and ethnic groups. When we speak of "welshing" on a deal, or "jewing down" or "gypping" someone, or riding in a "paddy wagon," we're using terms that are likely to give offense to some people.

Aryan Nation, so-called skinheads, and other "hate" groups reinforce the use of offensive language, names, and symbols (such as the Nazi swastika) as a way to promote their one-race agenda.

Yet, in some cases, the use of epithets might be entirely innocent. When children say, "This toy was a gyp," they have no knowledge of its ethnic origin. They are using a word they simply don't understand. It's just as if a child repeats a four-letter profanity he heard in a movie—he is swearing, but he doesn't necessarily know what it means.

All communication contains an element of subjectivity, or pure opinion. One person might read a racist meaning into a comment while another would not. For example, an incident occurred at the University of Pennsylvania one semester. Five African-American sorority sisters were passing underneath the dormitory room of a white male freshman who was trying to study. Because they were making noise, the freshman shouted for them to keep it down, calling them "water buffalo." The girls filed a racial harassment complaint.

The student admitted making the water buffalo comment. "I didn't do anything wrong," he said. "This had nothing to do with their skin. It had to do with the noise they were making."

The student was summoned to meet with an official who investigates charges of racial harassment. She asked him whether he had "racist thoughts" when he made his water buffalo comment. He firmly denied having such thoughts. "I don't know why it

TESTING YOUR OWN ATTITUDES

In order to come to grips with your own attitudes about other races, you need to constantly examine your opinions and behaviors. Do any of these sound familiar?

- The thought of having an African-American as president makes me uncomfortable.

- I don't dislike African-Americans or Hispanics, but I'd prefer it if they didn't move next door.

- Science has proven that whites are the most intelligent race.

- Mrs. Jones says she'll vote for candidate X for mayor because he's white.

- Mrs. Arnold says she'll vote for candidate Y for mayor because he's African-American.

- The races should remain pure and unspoiled; interracial marriage should not be allowed.

All of the above statements could easily have come from someone who has racist attitudes. Does the image of an African-American president make you "uncomfortable?" For most people, racism comes in a more subtle form, such as the embarrassing gaffe or the patronizing compliment. As we have seen, even the most compassionate among us may harbor racist attitudes.

popped into my head, they were stomping and making a 'woo, woo' noise. It seemed to describe what they were doing," he said.

The investigator sided with the sorority women. The student was informed that to settle the matter, he would have to agree to write a letter of apology in which he acknowledges his inappropriate behavior, be put on

This school desegregation rally organized by citizens of Puerto Rican descent is a reminder of the constant struggles new immigrants have faced in dealing with stereotypes.

probation in his dormitory, and have a letter put in his student file noting a "violation of the code of conduct on racial harassment."

He refused to sign the settlement letter and instead demanded a hearing before a panel of students and faculty. The five sorority sisters eventually dropped their racial harassment complaint, charging the press and the school with having "failed us miserably."

Some of Penn's African-American students argued that the crackdown on shouted insults is long overdue. Whenever African-American students gather together, blatantly racist slurs are hurled from the windows, they claim. Many minorities, in fact, see these sort of comments as a common thread of racism throughout the university system, not far removed from words like "nigger" and "spic."

The best way to change this pattern that leads to thoughtless or insensitive remarks is to start with children, says one expert. Seemingly harmless words and expressions used by a parent can have a lasting impact on the thoughts and actions of a child. "If it can be built into the family lifestyle, where it's more natural, it isn't such an overwhelming task." Until people realize these words are offensive, they will not change their thinking.

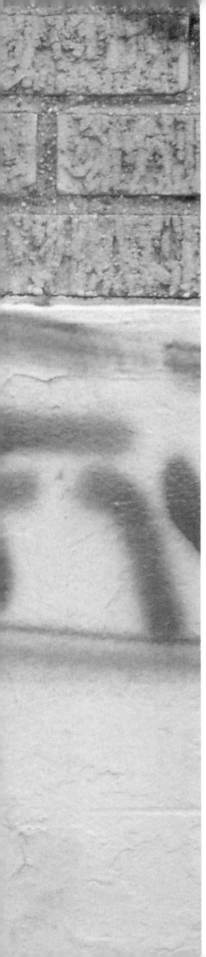

4

WHEN HATE TURNS VIOLENT

All I was doing was trying to get home from work.
— Rosa Parks, on refusing to move to the back of a bus.
Montgomery, Alabama, 1955.

Jermaine, an African-American high school student, was destined to be a great professional football player. Unfortunately, his career was cut short by a gang of white students. He was attending a party and talking to a white girl. He didn't know it at the time, but she happened to be the ex-girlfriend of one of the guys who was giving the party. "This guy got mad that she was 'talking to a nigger,'" remembers Jermaine. "We said a few things to each other, but I just brushed it off. I didn't think it was that big of a deal."

Later that evening, Jermaine sat on the board-walk with the same girl when a gang, some of whom belonged to the Skinheads, beat him on the head with aluminum baseball bats. They banged him more than a dozen times, then kicked him in the head before they ran away.

Jermaine was rushed to the hospital. He remained in a coma for several days. When he finally regained consciousness, he learned from the doctors that he might never play football again. He spent a long time in rehabilitation to relearn how to use his hands and legs. Even now, several years later, he still has problems seeing out of one eye and difficulty walking up steps—things he used to take for granted.

Hating people of other ethnic backgrounds, religions, and races is based upon ignorance and fear, and the inevitable result is often a violent assault on people and the destruction of property.

"There was always some racial tension on campus, but it never got out of hand," says Jermaine. "I was an athlete. I played on the same team as a lot of white guys. We would call each other names and stuff, but mostly it was light. The night I got beat up, I was just talking to a girl. She happened to be white, but we weren't even dating. We were just friends. The guys who hit me with baseball bats didn't even give me a chance to defend myself. They came up on me from behind. Now I've got to live with a handicap the rest of my life."

A 17-year-old student from Florida recalls his encounters with racism and violence. "Once on the way home from school, people started calling me 'kike' and 'dirty Jew,' and they chased me home," he explains. "I've had things thrown at me just because I was Jewish. One time, after a basketball game, when we were shaking hands, players from the other team just came up to us and called us 'dirty Jews' and started shoving us and punching us. I've been beaten up so many times, I've come to expect it every time I see a group of kids coming toward me."

A DISTURBING PICTURE

This kind of hate crime goes on all the time. A white woman was raped, shot five times in the head and dumped along the side of a road by five African-American men and two women in South Carolina who said they did it because of the 400 years of oppression of African-American people. In Southern California, a Korean-American grocer was convicted of voluntary manslaughter in the shooting of a 15-year-old African-American girl. The judge's decision to sentence the grocer to probation instead of prison, along with the acquittal of four police officers in the Rodney King beating trial, partially contributed, many believe, to the 1992 Los Angeles uprising.

More than 25 years ago, a government report on racism concluded that this country was divided into two societies—one African-American and one white—both separate and unequal, and that the primary cause "evolved from white racism." In 1991, Arthur Fletcher, then-chairman of the U.S. Civil Rights Commission, concluded that the U.S. is still a "racist nation" with the worst climate for civil rights in at least 40 years. Racism "is ingrained in our value system [and is] likely to be there for a long, long time," he said.

Prejudice can take the form of organized violence when promoted by hate or random violence. Consider, for example, the Crown Heights incident. On August 19, 1991, a station wagon driven by a Hasidic man swerved onto a sidewalk, running over and killing a seven-year-old African-American boy, Gavin Cato. Three hours later, a young Jewish scholar named Yankel Rosenbaum was surrounded by a group of African-American youths and stabbed. Four days of rioting, firebombing, and demonstrations followed.

Neighborhoods in New York City from Bensonhurst and Crown Heights to Howard Beach became synonymous with ugly racial incidents in the early 1990s. Neighbor shouted at neighbor during many days of marching and protests.

Members of racial and cultural groups often face physical dangers when they enter certain neighborhoods. In the 1980s, the words Bensonhurst and Howard Beach—names of all-white neighborhoods in New York City—became symbols of racial prejudice when African-Americans passing through the area were killed as a result of white violence. In 1991, the Los Angeles Police Department's excessive use of force on Rodney King became a nationwide scandal, as reports revealed that African-American people were routinely harassed in white neighborhoods.

Why is there this much hate in the world? How is it possible to heal profound wounds within and between ethnic groups when we're too busy killing each other? Cross-burning, racial slurs, a brick thrown through the window of an African-American family's home in an all-white neighborhood, and police brutality have become familiar symbols of the growing trend of racism and violence in our society.

HATE GROUPS

Hate groups that promote prejudice, discrimination, and violence have been around for a long time. The Ku Klux Klan was organized to suppress African-Americans in the years after the Civil War. The Klan was formed by white people who felt threatened by African-American people, Jewish-Americans, American Indians, and other minority groups. Klan members dressed in white robes and hoods so that they could not be recognized in their illegal activities. The organization continues to function today and is still strong in some communities.

Another major hate group is the American Nazi Party, inspired in the 1930s by the rise of the Nazi party of Germany. This group believes that an international Jewish conspiracy is responsible for all of America's problems, and that African-Americans are genetically inferior to white people. Throughout the 1970s and 1980s, other hate groups in the U.S. began to store firearms and other weapons with the plan of someday staging a military takeover, or, in some cases, defending themselves against those they fear will attack them.

If these groups are left alone to peddle their hate, racism will get worse. A poll by the American Jewish Committee, for example, found that 22 percent of Americans doubt that the Holocaust and the Nazi extermination of Jewish people even happened. Some scholars suggest this growing movement could seriously block efforts to improve race relations.

Simply dismissing these charges is not enough. Education is not enough, according to Kenneth S. Stern, author of *Holocaust Denial*. People who deny the existence of the holocaust must be confronted and exposed as frauds. "Holocaust denial is not about historical truth," he says. "It is about anti-Jewish hatred—and must be confronted as such."

One hate group that's been confronted, and the one with which you may be most familiar, is the Skinheads. Some people pass off these fanatics as merely thugs. Others claim they're much more organized and deadly. In July of 1993, for example, David Fisher, a 20-year-old former Boy Scout from Long Beach, California, was charged as the mastermind in a neo-Nazi plot to bomb the First African Methodist Episcopal Church in South Central Los Angeles. The group had hoped to ignite a "race war."

Fisher and two of his comrades were among eight suspected white supremacists arrested on weapons charges. Fisher's alleged campaign of terrorism also included plans to assassinate Rodney King and other prominent African-American and Jewish figures.

The leader of the 8,500-member church, Rev. Cecil L. Murray, said of the terrorist plot: "This is a symptom of where we are going if we don't arrest the flow of racism. When the economy is bad, morality tends to become bad, so that the hate-mongers emerge."

The oldest "hate" group in the United States, the Ku Klux Klan, still surfaces periodically to protest what they view as the decline of white rule.

Rev. Murray's Sunday message reflected hope. "In this lovely city, we have 146 different nations. We must learn how to walk together, children; we must learn how to love together...there's enough room for everybody."

The others who were arrested in Fisher's race war plan included a "yuppie" couple from the San Fernando Valley in Southern California. She was an accounting manager for a real estate office and he was a airline flight engineer.

Fisher, however, surprised even his friends. He lived with his parents and worked in a sandwich shop. One friend who had known Fisher since kindergarten said that there was nothing to suggest he had become a bigot with so much hate that he was willing to kill. According to an FBI undercover agent, however, he was the leader of a group of neo-Nazi types whose membership fluctuated between 18 and 40 people.

Fisher came to a point in his life where he felt he needed to protect white people. He viewed himself as a victim of reverse discrimination because his school established special events to help promote racial understanding of minorities, but not of whites. His parents tried to teach him the difference between having pride in one's race and bigotry. They even tried to get him to attend race awareness events, but without success.

Fisher couldn't understand why the high school had special days for minorities, from Cinco de Mayo to Black Pride Day, but nothing for whites. So during his first year in college, he founded the White Youth Alliance that was dedicated to white pride. He later established a more violent group called the Fourth Reich Skinheads. One friend said he was more pro-white than he was anti-black.

Are any of your friends members of a hate group like the Fourth Reich Skinheads? People who join these organizations are lost and confused. They need the strength of numbers to build their self-esteem. Unfortunately, most members of hate groups end up in trouble. One way to avoid trouble is to not hang around these groups. If you have friends who are members, encourage them to walk away.

Gangs can also be considered hate groups, if they're formed for racial reasons. Jeff, for example, was recently beat up by a gang of African-American students for walking through the wrong neighborhood. "They looked at me and all they saw was a white person," he says. "Now if I see a group of black kids coming toward me, I walk on the other side of the street just to protect myself. I'm just looking out for myself."

Louis Negrete is the senior leader of United Neighborhoods Organization (UNO) in East Los Angeles. This church-based organization trains people for leadership roles in their communities to participate in politics and public affairs. Its Hope in Youth campaign helps knit together groups of mothers and fathers who want to do something about gangs.

The reasons young people join gangs are many and complex, but inevitably gangs are divided along racial lines, and the competition for drug money and neighborhood "turf" leads to a racially-based "us verses them" attitude.

"Eighty percent of the gang wanna-bes can be helped," says Negrete. "In these critical times, when there's less public funding for programs, racism is stimulated and let loose, and it appears in many forms. Gangs and race relations in general are really questions of power. When people feel isolated by race and are made to feel powerless, we have problems. We try to counteract it by contributing to multiracial efforts, bringing together leaders from various ethnic communities and religions."

THE LOS ANGELES RIOTS

The streets were on fire in Los Angeles in 1992 after the first trial in the Rodney King beating trial ended in acquittals. More than 50 people died, and at least $800 million worth of property was destroyed during one of the worst civil disturbances in modern American history.

Was Rodney King a convicted felon resisting arrest, or the unfortunate target of a racially motivated assault by Los Angeles police officers? A federal court found two officers guilty of violating King's civil rights, two years after a devastating riot was set off because another jury found them not guilty of assault.

Shortly after the verdicts came down, a Korean-American liquor store was looted and the store owner's son was hit on the head. A crowd gathered and moved on to attack white, Asian, and Hispanic motorists. Around 6:45 p.m., truck driver Reginald Denny was pulled from his truck and beaten. Media attention took this one attack as a symbol of the violence, much like the African-American community took the image of Rodney King's beating as a symbol of racism. South Central Los Angeles became an inferno. National Guardsmen were stationed everywhere. Said one African-American person involved in the riots: "The verdict said to me the life of a black person has no value." The violence continued for three days.

A week after the riots, a Korean student watched his friend get shot in the leg by a African-American teenager while the friend defended his family's store during the riots.

"I came here with my mother in 1981," he says. "We lived in a studio apartment with rats and roaches. With the grace of God, we were able to move up the rungs of the ladder. A lot of African-Americans are condescending because they were born here and we are immigrants. If anything, we are more American than the African-American community because we earned it. We came here seeking American democracy. African-Americans say they were forced to come here because of slavery. If you don't like it, leave. Go back to Africa."

An English teacher at a California college held a class meeting after the riots. "We had a stormy discussion of the events," he says. "Many of the white students didn't understand what prompted people to burn and loot in their own communities."

The class was racially mixed. In early sessions, the students were asked to write compositions on a subject of their choice. Many wrote about racism and violence. "As some of the black students pointed out, African-Americans have suffered oppression," the professor says.

He described one Irish woman in his class who had two daughters from her marriage to an African-American man. She spoke about how she feels the rage build up inside her when she's standing in a playground and some white woman asks, "Who do those jungle bunnies belong to?" She told the class it makes her so mad that she feels like grabbing the woman by the neck and squeezing.

The question was frequently raised: Why are they burning their own neighborhoods? A number of African-American students felt the burning was selective. They tried to explain how there was also a large reservoir of anger left over from the killing of the black teenaged girl by the Korean-American grocer, as well as the Rodney King decision.

Eyebrows were raised when the African-American students said they felt white students weren't in touch with reality when it comes to racism. The white students said they felt African-American students weren't as "forthcoming" as they should be.

"Overall, the discussions were healthy and productive," says the professor. "This group had been together most of the semester and they jelled reasonably well. There wasn't as much anger as I thought there might have been. They had respect for each other, for the classroom, and for their instructor.

"It's helpful to have cross-cultural communication," he adds, "especially when there's a larger social issue that has a direct relationship with race relations.

Gang violence is commonplace in many American cities, and young people are most often the perpetrators and the victims. Members of the Boston group Gang Peace are trying to discourage this trend by speaking to those most affected by gang activity.

Students feel a need to communicate with each other. Students feel they are gaining a better understanding of the issues, and that's crucial, because that's what the business of education is all about."

After class, some of the students continued their discussion of the week's events. The professor felt as though they wanted to understand what contributed to the riots. They wanted to develop some kind of understanding of the issues and how history and current events had a direct relationship with one of the biggest social upheavals in the history of American cities.

"Their attempts to rise above the personal feelings and anxieties was a healthy kind of desire to learn the truth about race relations. I felt that once they were able to air their feelings, they could go back to their daily struggle to survive, but with a little more hope."

One white woman came up to the professor after class and said she was having trouble coming up with a subject for her next composition. He suggested she write about her police community relations, since her father was a police officer. "Maybe you should interview him," he offered. She said she couldn't, because her father had been shot and killed by a 13-year-old gang member several years earlier.

The next semester, that same woman was in the professor's creative writing class. "She sat next to a black woman who lost her son to a gang shooting. "They ended up becoming friends because they each had lost a loved one to urban violence. For me, that represented a kind of personal bridge that has to be built consistently between people, regardless of race, color, or class. The violence in this society will hurt all of us, unless we can figure out how to address it. Perhaps this exercise in class discussion was one small step."

FOR BETTER OR WORSE

During the riots, a *Los Angeles Times* photographer snapped a picture of a six-year-old African-American child making an obscene gesture toward the police, the middle finger of his left hand thrust high in the air. When his mother saw the picture in the newspaper, she decided to teach her son a lesson. She wrote a letter to the newspaper and invited a reporter to get to know her only child. "My son made a statement," said his mother. "I'm going to complete it." The reporter's story described one little boy's life in Los Angeles—his fear of ricocheting bullets, his love of soccer, his fierce devotion to his mother. It told how, during the riots, his mother used some of her meager income to buy her son a new toy, hoping he wouldn't become a looter. He seemed to respond to her gesture.

He wasn't the only one who found some good in the aftermath of the riots. Last spring, when Octavio Sandoval found a hard floor easier to sleep on than a guilty conscience, he made himself a local hero by returning three beds he had stolen during the riots. Dozens of caring citizens responded to his story; 30 people offered him beds. His story seemed a comforting close to a trying chapter in the city's history.

Octavio was a decent teenager who had been swept up in the moment and stolen something he and his family genuinely needed: beds to sleep on. Waiting to aid him were dozens of citizens who cared enough to help him and his family rest easier. Today, Octavio remains a symbol. Like hundreds of teenagers in the city, he's a youth who didn't make the honor roll, but he didn't join a gang, either. "I think I'm average," he replied when asked how he sees himself.

Average people can do extraordinary things when confronted with bad times. That's what it takes to overpower the hate and violence that comes with racism. Every day after lunch since the riots, a school bus picks up a 16-year-old student in Watts and takes her six blocks to a two-year course in consumer electronic repair. Her hope is for a technician job upon graduation from high school, a rare bright spot in glum post-riot Los Angeles. Here, 28 inner-city high school students are being given a chance to construct careers out of the ashes because of what one company, Pioneer Electronics, did with uncommon speed.

Five days after the riots, executives of the Tokyo-based corporation spent $600,000 to begin a job-training program, which meets for three hours each afternoon at a public housing project. Pioneer has promised the students summer internships and jobs if they stay on course. Many students have embraced the opportunity. The academy opened its doors in September 1992. The enrollment goal was 30 high school students per year. It was done with the cooperation of both private and public funds.

"When we met with community leaders to discuss ways in which Pioneer could help rebuild Los Angeles, the number one problem identified was joblessness," says Setsujiro Onami, president of Pioneer. "Through our expertise in electronics, we were able to provide vocational and job training in one of the most dynamic, fast-growing industries in the United States."

One teenager in the program moved to Los Angeles from Mexico. Her father is a material handler, her mother a housewife. She and her six brothers and sisters live in a home in the inner city. Before a counselor approached her, she had never thought about electronics, though she hoped to attend college. The Pioneer program intrigued her. "It sounded interesting, a chance to learn something," she says. "Before the riots, there was no progress." Now she is optimistic about her city's future.

Several other companies poured money into the inner city. Security Pacific/Bank of America, for example, started a program to help small businesses obtain loans with low rates. Southern California Edison developed job training centers at its vacant facilities. Litton Industries donated money for educational and social service programs.

Instead of turning to violence, citizens, businesses, and even some students have begun to rethink their own personal relations with others of different races.

CAN WE ALL GET ALONG?

The Civil Rights Movement brought about profound legal changes for minorities. These changes can be seen through legislation and court actions. Schools had to be integrated, minorities had to be treated the same as whites at public places likes stores and lunch counters, and racial discrimination in employment was outlawed. Although vast gains have been made, some minority groups still face discrimination and prejudice—and violence continues to be widespread and growing.

Racial tensions have been flaring at schools throughout the country. Students come to blows over the type of music played at a homecoming dance, while their parents compete against each other for jobs. A way out does exist. Jin, 17, is a Korean immigrant and student body president at his high school. He lives in Los Angeles with his mother, who recently opened a small store.

RACE RELATIONS IN ONE AMERICAN CITY

According to a 1992 poll on attitudes about race relations, we've made little progress in learning to get along with people of a color or race different from our own.

• *How would you rate race relations in Los Angeles?*

	Whites	Black	Hispanics	Asians
Excellent	1%	1%	—	5%
Good	12%	16%	20%	20%
Not so good	42%	40%	45%	53%
Poor	43%	42%	35%	18%
Don't know	2%	1%	—	4%

• *Do you think race relations in Los Angeles are getting better or worse?*

	Whites	Black	Hispanics	Asians
Getting better	12%	10%	18%	24%
Getting worse	42%	39%	38%	25%
Staying the same	42%	49%	43%	51%
Don't know	4%	2%	1%	—

• *These days, do you think racism is mainly something white people are guilty of in America or are other groups guilty of racism as well?*

	Whites	Black	Hispanics	Asians
White people	3%	9%	6%	4%
Other groups as well	95%	88%	92%	87%
Don't know	2%	3%	2%	9%

• *How close are we to eliminating discrimination against African-Americans and other minorities in America?*

	Whites	Black	Hispanics	Asians
Close	17%	10%	29%	26%
Not close	79%	90%	70%	73%
Don't know	4%	—	1%	1%

Source: The Los Angeles Times.

Taking time to learn about our fellow classmates is one important step to making peace on our campuses and in our neighborhoods.

He hopes to attend college in the fall. "Despite the unrest, my mom and I are committed to staying here," he says. "We weren't hurt. At the time, we really had nothing to lose. Also, being from Korea, where there is so much war and poverty, my mom and many Korean people think that violence is just part of life.

"I think Koreans got hurt for a reason. We have too many leaders and not enough followers. A lot of Koreans view themselves as leaders. They don't always listen to people. They always want to do what they want to do, what's best for them, for their interests. I have to change myself first. When people say, 'Oh, this group did this and that group did that,' it makes me angry. We have to look first at what we did wrong. If we can't do that, if we can't change, how can we ask someone else to change?

"You have to be willing to change," he continues. "When we speak Korean, everyone else thinks we are saying something bad about them. I think you have to give a little to get something back. There are not enough people willing to give. And even those people who want to give often don't know where or how to start. I try to be optimistic, but I don't see that there's any way we can get better, unless every one just wakes up and changes everything in society—how the media works, how people think. We have to start paying attention to racial differences, but we also have to stop using them as an excuse for not doing anything. We have to stop thinking about where we came from or what happened to our great-great-grandfathers. We have to figure out what we are going to do with our lives. We should stop focusing on where we've come from or the color of our skin. We need to think about where we're going from here."

Leslie, 16, is a senior at a private school and was a youth leader of last year's interracial project. She hopes to attend law school. "At my school, it's always them and their problems. It's never us and our problems. And yet these are problems that we all have to figure out how to solve.

"There needs to be more direct contact between those who are privileged and those who are not," she continues. "There are too many people who don't have the basic human necessities, and there are even more people who turn their heads and pretend problems don't exist. I'm guilty of that, too. Just now, I saw a homeless man on the street. This man doesn't even have a place to live, and I do nothing to help him. As individuals, we need to stop what we are doing and help. We need to start demanding that our government address these problems."

5

RACISM IN SCHOOL

It is never too late to give up our prejudices.
— Henry David Thoreau
Economy [1854]

Tad is one of the few African-American students in the drama department at his high school in Arizona. He wants to be a professional actor like Denzel Washington. Unfortunately, it's hard for him to get roles in his high school productions because he's African-American. The school always performs plays with "white" roles. The rejection has made him question his own abilities. "Is it me, or is it because I'm black?" he asks. "I'm getting good grades in performance class, but I can't land a good part."

Last month, Tad finally broke new ground when he landed the lead role in his school's production of Shakespeare's Macbeth. "It gave me the confidence I needed to continue to pursue my dream," he says, "and it gave me strength to not let racism get in my way of going to the top."

Lynn is a 16-year-old Chinese-American woman. "The other students think I'm brilliant, good at math, and that I'm submissive and passive," she says. "But I'm not that good in math, and I don't consider myself passive. What hurts the most is that a large number of my peers don't even see me as an American, even though I was born here. I grew up on Sesame Street. I speak perfect English. But I look different, and they think all Asians are alike."

Almost all new groups of immigrants to the United States encounter some stereotyping. Many people assume that all Asian-Americans are "good at math," and generally achieve higher grades in school, for example.

Mike is a 17-year-old white student from New York. "I'm not safe from persecution in the classroom," he says. "I feel we spend more time in my history class talking about what whites owe blacks than just about anything else. I often get dirty looks. This seems strange given that I wasn't even alive then. The few members of my family who were around during slavery didn't have the luxury of owning much, let alone slaves. So why, I ask you, am I constantly made to feel guilty? I don't hate blacks or any other minority group, so why does everyone think I do?"

These are issues and questions students across the country are raising. Racism in school can be found in your drama department, in sports, or in your classmates or teachers. Just look around you. Is there an African-American student in your drama department who's feeling the same way as Tad? Does your coach make racial jokes during practice? Does your peer group exclude a certain class of people? Are you feeling overwhelmed with the whole issue of racism?

As American society grows more diverse, students are getting caught in the middle. Many American students still are affected by institutional racism. One school district in Illinois, for example, placed black and white children in separate classrooms as recently as 1993.

The school district was allegedly desegregated—that is, forced by law to allow minority groups to equally share facilities and activities with the majority—during the 1970s and 1980s. But several schools in Rockford weren't playing by the same rules. Black and white students, for example, ate at separate lunch times and used separate bathrooms. Hispanic students, traveling to schools in white neighborhoods, were forced to stay on their school buses before morning classes, while local white children were allowed to play football and basketball in the school yard.

One Hispanic former student in Rockford recalls as an eight-grader having to get up at 6:30 in the morning to make the long commute to school by bus. "The bus arrived 15 to 20 minutes before the school building opened every day, but we had to remain on board while the white students were on the playground," he recalls. "The principal told us we were lucky to have a ride. He said if we didn't like it, we should walk." African-American students were also forced to wait on buses before school.

Are other school districts avoiding the issue of integration by finding their own creative solutions to the problems facing a multi-ethnic student body? It seems so, and the Rockford case may just be the tip of the iceberg.

One district official described Rockford's schools as "a system of apartheid," the name for the official policy of segregation and economic discrimination practiced until recently in South Africa.

As a result, most white students went into honors and college-prep classes, while minority students—some of whom scored high on academic

Desegregation, the legal policy that forces certain school districts to achieve racial balance, brings students from different racial and ethnic backgrounds together in classrooms like this one. Whether it eliminates racism itself is still open to debate.

tests—remained stuck in the slow-learner sections. The Rockford School District "has committed such open acts of discrimination as to be cruel," wrote a federal judge in his report, after a class-action suit was filed by a community group. The school district was accused of operating an unfair and unequal system, and of denying minority students their rightful educational opportunities.

The school's superintendent admitted that one system of learning existed for white students and another for minority students, but he blamed it on pressure from white parents and on officials who were oblivious to the effect of their actions. "None of it," he said, "sounds defensible."

A judge forced the school district to make changes that would guarantee minority students fair access to college preparatory and honors classes, and to extracurricular activities. "Nobody will be doing anything out of the goodness of their hearts," said one African-American parent. "I do know that we will have to be constantly watching."

Documented accounts of public slurs, threats, racist slogans, physical assaults, and racial conflicts now ring disturbingly from schools in every region of the country. One expert claims that racism, prejudice, and discrimination are "shamefully sabotaging" our nation's effort to provide a high-quality education for all students. Yet education is our only hope for breaking the chains of racism.

These days, it's not enough just to go to school, without a clear and distinctive opinion on race relations. If you're serious about doing your part, you can start by taking a long, hard look at the issues that affect your daily life. Adult concepts like multiculturalism and affirmative action may sound intimidating, but how you concern yourself with these issues may determine your future.

MULTICULTURALISM

Whether you're in elementary school or a university, you need to know about the heritage and contributions of people of African descent, Asian descent, Latin American descent, as well as people of European descent. Multiculturalism is the label given to this new movement in education. This notion states that ethnic and cultural groups in the United States should respect their identities instead of diffusing and merging them in a melting pot.

Some people claim that our schools have been dominated for far too long by the attitudes, the beliefs, and the value system of one race and one class of people. By including the stories and histories of others in a multicultural setting, students can learn to avoid racism and appreciate cultural diversity, thus building pride in many ethnic identities.

Esther Taira, for example, is developing a multicultural curriculum for the Los Angeles City Unified School District. "We need to begin to look at the harder issues that confront students today," she says. "The issue of diversity is much more pronounced. We have yet to figure out exactly how to address this issue in our formal education setting."

Taira's program is a response to requests from a group of African-American students who came forward and said, "We don't feel equipped to deal with these issues. We want our education to include these kinds of things."

The issue of black-white in the Los Angeles City Unified School District, she says, is over-simplistic. "We're talking about this whole issue of their own voices and images being portrayed in history, from the history books they read to the literary works," says Taira. "They want to see themselves in the fabric of society."

Another issue they wanted brought to the table was the human factor. Coming from diverse backgrounds, these students wanted to know how they could more positively relate to one another. Third, these students wanted to find the tools to become participating members of society.

"This is a collaborative effort between students, the district, and the community," says Taira. "We can't expect a quick fix or something that will be

These students at Eastern District High School in Brooklyn, New York, are attending an assembly on multiculturalism.

resolved by a two-day summit meeting. We have to be in there for the long haul. We have to understand that what we're looking to do is worth doing right. If we can just learn to acknowledge our differences, we can then work on creating an atmosphere that will allow for bridge building and collaboration."

Students and teachers are asking themselves these questions: Why aren't the contributions of people of color found in history books? How come students can't relate to each other's differences? What sort of tools are necessary to become positive members of society?

In the past, history books have taught only that European-Americans have contributed to this country. White students quickly accepted the idea that they were in the superior position among their peers. They became oblivious to all but the most blatant acts of racism or ethnic discrimination and often re-labeled such acts as cultural differences or political advantage. Students of color, by contrast, were separated from their roots. Yet they felt the need to examine their own experiences and history, and relate it to other groups.

If society won't do it, schools must try to communicate truth and reality—of telling the complete story of history and human experience. As one teacher puts it, "... we need to incorporate into the curriculum another story, a nonwestern story of the world. Students need to view concepts, themes, issues, and problems from several ethnic perspectives."

Is multiculturalism the answer? Some educators say that past efforts to teach multiculturalism may have widened the ethnic divisions they were meant to close. In one school, most students felt happy and proud when they celebrated holidays or held appreciation days for their ethnic groups. Few students raised their hands when asked whether they remembered discussing the culture of a different ethnic group, however. Experts say that most students tend to take only those classes that relate to the group to which they belong. In such a climate, even the celebration of ethnic holidays has caused problems, with one group believing that another has received more attention. Some groups actually boycott another group's festivities. "On Martin Luther King Day, they were celebrating black people," says an Hispanic tenth-grader. "I went to the event, but none of the people were of my color. I felt all alone."

The current approach in schools, which relies largely on ethnic studies courses and the recognition of special holidays and heroes, may be isolating students from each other. Can we study ourselves as separate groups? Certainly, our paths as members of different groups crisscross each other. Some young people have misunderstood lessons about ethnic pride, developing instead an attitude of ethnic superiority.

"We do have ethnic-specific courses, but they do not create the bridges we need," says Taira, whose course is an elective offered only in some select schools. "Even when we do talk about more than one group, we tend to focus on similarities, and that ignores the problems in the streets. Their differences are the issues."

IN THE CLASSROOM

How can you make your classroom a safe environment for people of all races, cultures, and religions? Here are just a few suggestions:

(1) Be honest about your opinions of other races. This may help open the lines of communication with teachers and students, and it may answer some of your questions.
(2) Make the effort to learn about each other's cultures and religions. Ask questions of students who come from different backgrounds.
(3) When discussing issues of race in the classroom, be sure to set clear guidelines on how to address one another and how to be honest without being rude.
(4) Find new ways to understand your own attitudes and behaviors.
(5) Learn as much as you can about racism and how it works.
(6) Agree to purge your speech of racial and ethnic slurs and jokes.
(7) Pledge to act as individuals against racist behavior.

WHAT ABOUT TEACHERS?

Every time a teacher or a person in authority fails to confront racist attitudes, behaviors, and ideas among students, he or she is contributing to an unhealthy environment not only for students of color, but for all students. Students can notice and even take offense when they see a teacher treat some students differently than others.

"At my school, there are a lot of blacks," says one 14-year-old white student. "Black students, black teachers, and a black principal. There is a lot of discrimination in the classroom. If a black kid does something wrong in a black teacher's class, he gets off easy. If a white kid does the same thing, he gets into big trouble. I think that blacks should feel lucky that now they have their freedom and whites have helped them get there. Blacks should learn to show the same respect to whites that they show to their own people. Blacks and whites should respect one another equally."

Certainly, reverse discrimination exists. White students can be treated unfairly just as easily as minority students. This practice is called a double standard, a set of principles that applies differently to one group of people than to another. Many minority students, for example, may believe that teachers think they aren't as prepared for college work as white students. They may also

Teachers are important role models for students, and how students are treated in the classroom has much to do with their attitudes toward race.

believe that the teachers expect less of them and thus evaluate them differently because of it. If you feel you're being treated unfairly, or if you feel you're being evaluated on a different scale than the other students in your class, talk to a counselor or the principal—maybe he or she can do something about it.

Success in school is strongly related to self-esteem. Studies show that African-American students, especially those of low socio-economic status, tend to have lower self-esteem than white students. School is certainly one place where self-pride and confidence can and should be instilled in young people as an ongoing part of the educational process. Students have a right to grow and experience their dreams. We must celebrate differences, and treat everyone with respect.

RACISM IN SPORTS

M elissa used to love to swim. When she was a child, her grandfather would take her and her brothers swimming at a local pond in the backwoods near where they lived in Mississippi. He used to tell her stories about how when he was a child his grandfather would teach him how to swim, and how he became the best swimmer in the entire county. Melissa remembers the feel of the cool water on her body during a hot summer's day, as her grandfather taught her first how to dog paddle, and then the breast stroke. She wanted to be the best swimmer in the entire county—like her grandfather.

When Melissa entered high school back in the 1980s, she tried out for the girls' swimming team. Although it took a lot of hard work and practice, she made the team in her junior year. "I was so excited when I found out I had made the team," she recalls. "After school that day, I rode my bike as fast as I could to my grandfather's house and told him the good news. He started to cry."

She was the first African-American student in her school to ever make the girls' swimming team.

The first swim meet was held at a local country club in another part of town. Melissa didn't realize it at the time, but it was a country club that excluded African-Americans. She noticed some of the officials talking with her coach. "I didn't know what was going on, so I looked up at my grandfather sitting proudly in the bleachers. He just smiled at me."

Melissa's coach walked over and told her the news: She was not allowed to participate in the swim meet because it was being held at a segregated country club. Her school went ahead and competed without her. "I just looked up at my grandfather, stunned. I could tell he wanted to cry, but he didn't. It wasn't fair. I had earned my spot on that team, and I should have been able to compete."

Melissa later talked to her grandfather about the incident at the country club. "He told me a story about how Jackie Robinson broke the color barrier in major league baseball, and how he opened the door to professional sports for other African-American athletes. He said I had opened doors for other high school athletes. It made me feel better, but I'm still angry about it. It was so unfair."

Life can be unfair. Although discrimination is illegal in public settings, private clubs still have the option to exclude whomever they choose. This is a more subtle form of racism that can be just as harmful as the more obvious kind. Often the only way to deal with this sort of racism is to stand up for your rights.

THE GREAT EQUALIZER

Sports like baseball, basketball, football, and swimming should be free of racism. But life, even on the playing field, isn't always fair. Melissa broke the color barrier at her school, but she couldn't compete at a segregated country club. Similar experiences by high school students around the country have led some to believe that sports do not always lead to equality of opportunity for all races.

In 1979, for example, a fifteen-year-old African-American football player who had just caught a pass that gave his team a 6-0 half-time lead was shot by a sniper as his team gathered in a huddle before the second half. It was assumed that the shots were fired in reaction to a court-ordered busing plan that had placed Boston at the center of racial hatred and violence. The student later said: ". . . I think they were trying to kill somebody black, not wound somebody black, not make somebody black paralyzed; their intention was to kill somebody black."

At another high school in North Carolina just a few years ago, a cross was burned during the half-time festivities of a football game between a team of black students and a team of white students. Charges of racism also dominated a 1989 football season in South Carolina when a local coach replaced a black quarterback (who led his team to a winning record the year before) with a quarterback who was white. Thirty black players quit the squad.

One of the mistaken assumptions about race and sports is that athletic contact between blacks and whites will naturally change racial perceptions for the better, says Richard Lapchick, author of *Five Minutes to Midnight: Race and Sport in the 1990s.* "It has now become clear to me that for this change to take place, you need leaders both on and off the fields."

Lapchick believes these leaders can help bring students together through sports. The Reebok study on youth attitudes on racism, for example, showed that a majority of high school students reported that they had become friends with someone from a different racial or ethnic group through playing sports. By continuing these friendships off the field, athletes become role models for other students.

The system, however, isn't always fair. Black athletes have a harder time graduating from high school than white athletes. Black athletes are over-represented

Going to a good school on an athletic scholarship and making it in the pros is the dream of many athletes—a dream that comes true for very few.

in basketball and football, but only 10 percent receive athletic scholarships. On campus, black athletes are sometimes separated from other black students. Black student-athletes have unrealistic expectations of making the pros (44 percent believe they will make it, versus the 1 in nearly 8,000—or less than one percent—of high school athletes who actually do). All this amounts to a sports system that has helped break down racial barriers, but it has not been enough to wipe out racism in sports.

IT TAKES TEAMWORK

If sports are going to help promote brotherhood and sisterhood, and equality of opportunity for all races, then continued changes are critical. Ever since Jackie Robinson became the first African-American player to be signed by a major league baseball club, sports have come to symbolize teamwork among players of different races. Sport contacts with other nations build friendships, peace, and understanding. Sports have helped lead African-Americans out of the ghetto through increased educational opportunity, changing attitudes of white teammates and opponents, and increased employment opportunities for African-American athletes.

Especially now, as racial violence in our society appears to be increasing (hate crimes alone have increased 149 percent since 1987), sports are an excellent way to better race relations. Whether you're an athlete on your school team or just a supporter, you can help make sports a better place for all races:

- *Ask your parents to attend sporting events.* Experts believe that the more interest parents take in their children's lives, the more likely their children are to participate in honest and worthy activities like football, basketball, and baseball.
- Even if you're not a good athlete, *try out for a school team instead of joining a gang.* Athletes tend to hang around other athletes—who are less likely to become involved in gang activities and drugs.
- *Avoid violence before, during, and after a sporting event.* Be a good sport, even if your team loses.

You can learn a lot from sports. They teach the virtues of self-discipline, hard work, competitive spirit, and pride in accomplishment. They provide lessons about limits and capabilities, winning and losing, teamwork and cooperation. These lessons can be transferred into other areas of your life. They can be used to make you and others better students and better citizens of the community.

AFFIRMATIVE ACTION

Roger lives in Little Rock, Arkansas. Last summer, he waited eagerly for his acceptance letter from a prestigious college on the East coast. Unfortunately, it never came. "I know why I didn't get in that college," he says. "It's because I'm white. No one is going to do anything for me, affirmative-action wise. If I had been black, or Hispanic, or American Indian, I would be attending my first class. Hey! I've got the same problems they do, except I'm white. I feel I'm being discriminated against. I don't like affirmative action or quotas, but that doesn't make me a racist."

Many students will be attending college someday. Are affirmative action programs cause for concern?

For more than two centuries, minorities have suffered from the effects of discrimination in employment and education. They were denied jobs because of the color of their skin. They were forced into schools that were separate and unequal. In an effort to fix the situation, the federal government established affirmative action guidelines to ensure fairness and that applicants were employed without regard to their race, creed, color, or national origin.

Some people say affirmative action is a necessary approach because without it, racial discrimination in employment and education would continue

Will children of diverse ethnic and racial backgrounds be helped or hindered by affirmative action policies as they grow older? School admissions policies and business hiring practices that use specific guidelines to achieve balance continue to be challenged in the courts.

unchecked. Others argue that it does more harm than good. While it may help some people, it also makes them feel as though they've been hired simply because they are members of a minority, not because of their qualifications.

"I don't think white people owe anything to black people," says Jana, a junior from Montana. "We didn't sell them into slavery, our ancestors did. What they did was wrong, but we've done our best to make up for it. I think we are all equal. We shouldn't pay more attention to one race than the others. No race of people is superior to another. I think most people believe in 'equal' rights."

Janice, a senior from Michigan, has another perspective. "Whites owe blacks a great deal of respect and a place where they know they shouldn't feel any resentment," she says. "Giving a person a life that they can control themselves is the greatest gift a person can receive."

Many polls show that white citizens are more racially tolerant than they were several years ago, and that they support the rights of African-Americans and other minorities to have as good a chance as whites to get a job. But some white people in the U.S. are still deeply conflicted when it comes to affirmative action programs. They have a deep-seated feeling that these programs may eliminate discrimination against minorities, but at the expense of white citizens. This issue is complicated, and there are no easy answers.

What it comes down to is this: If we were all treated fairly, we wouldn't need affirmative action programs and quotas. The majority of whites believe blacks face little or no discrimination in employment, while most blacks believe just the opposite. Is everyone being treated fairly at your school? Are the teachers on campus mostly one race? Are some students receiving special attention because of the color of their skin? Is this good or bad? The important question is whether it's possible to arrive at a system that treats everyone fairly, regardless of skin color.

A WAR OF WORDS

In recent years, college campuses across the country have come up against an increasing number of harassment incidents. These have ranged from hate-filled graffiti and flyers to displaying Ku Klux Klan robes to African-Americans and shouting anti-Semitic insults at students.

For example, a fraternity at one university threw a "Fiji Island Party," with members wearing black painted faces. They set up a large caricature cutout of an African-American man with a bone through his nose. At another college, an African-American student hurled anti-Semitic insults, such as "dirty Jew" and "stupid Jew," at another Jewish student. These events can worsen racial tensions on campus, and lead to a "get even" mentality by others in the community. What can you do about it?

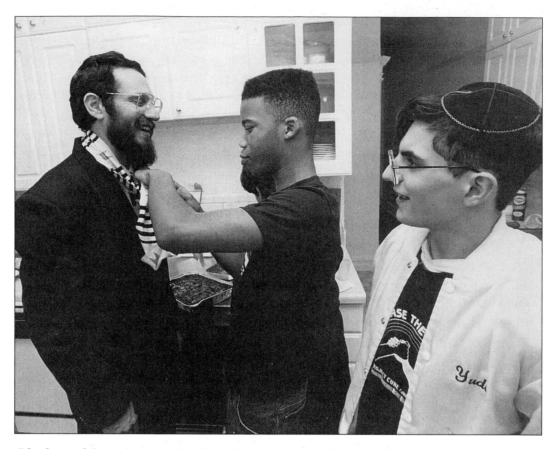

Blacks and Jews in America have had particularly tense relationships in the past decade. Community groups such as CURE (Communication Understanding Respect Education) are working hard to lower barriers and promote their "cure" for racism.

Some colleges have adopted anti-harassment conduct codes that impose an outright ban on offensive expression in certain contexts. For example, one university could expel students from class if they used disparaging names for other minorities or insensitive jokes, while another college might penalize students to a lesser degree for the same behaviors.

Some people claim these policies violate the First Amendment of the U.S. Constitution. What do you think? Should rules forbid racial insults and epithets? Should these rules apply to the choice of a guest speaker, or an article written by a professor? The First Amendment is often an important weapon for minorities as a means of spotlighting their grievances. Would you want your school to limit what you said on campus?

Students can actually make a difference by taking a stand on racism and discrimination. "We need to ban certain offensive speech on campus," says Michael, a high school senior from Georgia. "If somebody called me a 'wop,' it would make me mad, and I'd want to fight back. If I called a black student a 'nigger,' I would expect him to fight me. We can't just let students say whatever they feel. It would cause a lot more friction."

"I don't get it," says Stephanie, a high school junior from Minnesota. "They teach us in class about our freedoms, and then they try to put limits on what we say outside the classroom. It doesn't make sense. It's important to say what we feel. It's the first step in breaking down the barriers that now separate the races."

Racism stirs people's emotions in deep ways, and it's important to have the opportunity to bring about changes. Avoiding confrontation only allows bad situations to build to a boiling point. There needs to be a pressure valve to release some of the anger. Here are some responsible and effective ways to help decrease racism and discrimination on campus:

- Talk to your teachers and other students about your feelings;
- Get to know someone of another race;
- Write an article denouncing racism for the school newspaper;
- Write poems or stories that express your feelings;
- Read a book about an important person of another race;
- Attend multicultural activities with your friends.
- Organize a letter-writing campaign to local officials about your concerns over racism and discrimination.

6

FACE THE HATE

. . . [M]y religion makes me be against all form of racism. It keeps me from judging any man by the color of his skin. It teaches me to judge him by his deeds and his conscious behavior.
— Malcolm X
Speech, *Prospects for Freedom*, New York [1965]

Mark moved to Philadelphia from Idaho when he was 16 years old. Back home, he was considered an exceptional basketball player. He made the varsity team in his sophomore year. His new school, however, was well-known for producing talented players. Mark knew the competition to make the team would be tough, so he spent his summer practicing on the playgrounds.

Mark usually wore his lucky Boston Celtics shirt, which made him stand out even more in Philadelphia. During one hot afternoon of two-on-two competition, Mark almost came to blows with an African-American player everyone called Mo. "He started harassing me about being white and how I couldn't 'hang with the black' players," Mark recalls. "Everyone gets harassed when they're playing basketball, but this was different. He was attacking me on a personal level."

After the game, Mark went up to Mo and asked him if he had a problem. "I wanted to know if he was just harassing me or if he really didn't like white people," says Mark. "He took offense at my question and shoved me. I shoved him back and we got into a fight. A few of the guys separated us, but not before Mo called me white trash, and I called him a nigger."

Team sports can bring people together instead of separating them by race and by gang. It all depends upon the attitude each individual brings to the playing field.

Mark and Mo ran into each other several weeks later at a different basketball court; this time they were on the same team. "We played well together," says Mark. "In fact, we went undefeated for six games before we called it quits for lunch."

Over hamburgers and fries, Mark again asked Mo if he hated white people. "I learned that Mo didn't know that many white people, and that those he did know didn't like him because he was black," says Mark. "He just assumed I didn't like him because he was black. Once we got to know each other, we realized we had a lot in common. We made a great two-on-two team."

IT'S NEVER EASY

Racism is a tough subject to approach people with. We resist it because it's painful to discuss, especially in racially-mixed settings. One reason for the resistance, according to some experts, is that we're self-conscious about the subject, having been raised not to discuss it in public.

Children as young as three typically notice racial differences. Certainly, preschoolers talk about what they see. Unfortunately, they often do so in ways that make adults uncomfortable. Imagine the following scenario: A white child

These third graders are old enough to notice racial and ethnic differences. What they think and feel about those differences is learned from adults, and is therefore the most significant factor in reducing racism.

in a public place points to a dark-skinned African-American child and says loudly, "Why is that boy black?" The embarrassed parent quickly responds, "Shh! Don't say that." The child is only attempting to make sense of a new observation, yet the parent's attempt to silence the perplexed child sends a message that this observation is not okay to talk about. As a result, children learn not to ask questions about this topic.

Recognizing that we all have some prejudices and that many of us may benefit from discrimination against others is a useful first step in understanding racism. However, it's helpful to remember that once we understand how prejudice and discrimination work, we must find the right choices to combat them. "When I hear a racist remark, I feel like I should do something, but I don't know what," says a 17-year-old high school student. In fact, both individual and institutional change is possible, but understanding and unlearning prejudices and racism is a lifelong process.

REDUCING RESISTANCE

What are the everyday skills you need to be able to reduce the prejudice and racial conflicts that take place around you? One of the most important skills that you can use is to listen to someone, even when you strongly disagree with what that person is saying. It will be hard at first, so don't let your emotions get the better of you. It's only natural to be angry, for example, if someone's calling you a name, but step away from your emotions and listen to what the person is trying to say.

Another way to resolve conflict is to appreciate someone even when they say oppressive things that you do not like. "The most powerful way to change someone else's attitude is to give them a chance to hear a personal story," says Cherie Brown, founder of the National Coalition Building Institute (NCBI), a non-profit organization that holds prejudice reduction workshops on campuses throughout the country. "We can refute facts and figures, but we cannot ignore someone else's story. Only when they can claim pride in their own ethnicity can they get rid of their racism."

CLASSROOM TECHNIQUES FOR CHANGE

NCBI has one of the most effective programs in the country for reducing prejudices in students. The organization has put together a series of workshops where students learn how to become role models for other students, and how to take what they've learned about racism and train other students. If you want to organize such a class project, ask a popular teacher to help or contact NCBI.

One way of welcoming diversity: This pair are not related, but the woman is a Big Sister, part of the Big Brothers/Big Sisters of America program. Caring for another human being need not be hindered by racial differences.

The following are learning techniques you can use in school. Be sure to have a counselor or teacher moderate the sessions.

Forming stereotypes. NCBI recommends that students explore their thoughts about a particular ethnic group. Select a partner and choose a group to which neither of you belongs. This allows you the freedom to be honest with yourself and your partner without fear of making someone angry. Each student takes a turn saying the name of an ethnic group while the other partner, without hesitation, responds with uncensored thoughts. This process helps you to understand that everyone harbors negative impressions, and that no one person or group is singled out for blame.

Subconscious oppression. Most of us have no problems talking about prejudices of other groups, but when we're forced to address the prejudices against our own group, the process becomes much more painful. Select a partner who belongs to the same ethnic group as you. Point a finger at him or her and say, "What I can't stand about your race is . . ." For example, an Hispanic student might say, "What I can't stand about Hispanics is that they have too many children." According to NCBI, the negative thoughts one has about one's own group usually come from the prior negative stereotypes others have had about their group. Once you have aired the negative feelings about your own group, you can begin to express the positive. Return to the same partner, but this time express what you are proud of about your own ethnic group.

Recognizing oppression. NCBI believes that people have to be mistreated before they will mistreat others. For example, the boss yells at your father for making a mistake at work, your father comes home and yells at your mother for something silly, your mother yells at you to clean your room, and you yell at the dog.

Make a list of types of discrimination and prejudice. Then, break off into groups that have experienced the same injury or discrimination. Prepare a report for the whole class, responding to the question: "What do you never again want another person to say, think, or do to your group?"

Changing your attitude. The most effective way to break the chains of racism is through the sharing of personal stories, which tend to summon forth strong emotions and feelings. What NCBI has found is that many people are willing to share their pain and anger on a deep level. Often the listener is stirred to recall similar experiences.

"The benefits of personal storytelling are not only restricted to the listener," says Brown. "The storyteller also benefits in two principal ways. First, he or she gains a number of new, better-informed allies who are roused to fight against the oppression. Second, he or she can often heal the internal pain caused by the original injury."

Sharing of personal stories also helps the storyteller release the emotions that have often been buried since the initial incident occurred.

Changing your behavior. In trying to fight the battle of racism, you must start with the simplest of forms, usually the racial joke or slur. "These comments may not be the most institutionalized forms of discrimination, but they are often the most commonly experienced examples," says Brown.

When most people hear an oppressive comment, they usually respond in two ways. They either ignore the comment or put themselves into a defensive stance. Neither response is effective in changing attitudes and behavior. Instead of quickly acting to silence a person who makes a bigoted comment, ask respectful questions by using non-racist humor to break the ice, or simply through careful listening. Brown has noticed that participants who constantly interrupt bigoted remarks were more likely to also help stop institutionalized racism.

Maybe you're eating lunch with your friends and someone starts in with a racial joke. Instead of allowing the joke to continue, politely say that you're not interested and explain your reasons why. Or the next time someone starts spouting off about a particular ethnic group, listen carefully then ask respectful questions about his or her opinions. Try to get to the root of the person's prejudices.

Welcome diversity. There are many highly emotional issues in school, such as gangs, hate crimes, multiethnic relationships. One approach to overcoming these issues is to bring together some of the opposing groups and work toward a common goal. During these meetings, allow each person to explain his or her position, then ask the other person to repeat back with as much accuracy as possible what he or she heard. Next, have each person ask a clarifying question that will gather new information about the position of the other. Finally, ask the entire group for its reaction.

WHAT'S NEXT?

Exploring so much discrimination and unfairness, so many deep-seated stereotypes, can be upsetting, frightening, maddening, painful, and confusing. In order not to feel overwhelmed by what we have learned, we have to start finding ways of coping with our anger and pain.

Whether you are the target of prejudice, are someone who holds prejudices, or both, or even if you are just someone who is concerned about prejudice in society, how you respond will often determine the reaction you get from the other person. "The single concern that most people have is the sense of powerlessness," says Brown of NCBI. "Who am I to make a difference against all the oppression that's out there?"

One way to fight racism and the type of riots set off in Los Angeles is to learn about other ethnic groups. Take time to study and read about people like Malcolm X, who felt compelled to fight oppression. Getting some facts will help you avoid racist behavior and attitudes.

You can make a difference, even if it's in small doses:

- Read more about a particular ethnic group.
- See a movie focusing on different cultures.
- Attend a cultural event sponsored by a group different from your own.
- Make a resolution that whenever anyone expresses a remark that you consider prejudiced, you will speak up.
- Take a look at the activities you do regularly such as sports, drama, the school paper, clubs, hanging out with friends. Find some way you can broaden the range of who participates in these activities.
- Elect student body candidates who will oppose discrimination in all its forms.

LEARN TO HELP EACH OTHER

Not all students react positively to programs that try to help them come to grips with their own views about different races and cultures. Some respond negatively, some even with hostility. A lot depends on whether the program pressures students into admitting they are racists, says NCBI's Cherie Brown, who for more than 20 years has been a trainer in prejudice reduction workshops.

The most painful part of discrimination is the negative feelings we have about our own group, she adds. Hispanic students, for example, may be embarrassed by their parents because they speak limited English. "Anything negative we feel about our group is a hurt that needs to get healed," says Brown.

If students are forced to label themselves as racists, they can quickly become defensive and begin to resist the training. If prejudice-reduction programs are too tame, the hard issues never get raised and racism goes unchallenged. Perhaps the most effective way to face our own fears of the "other race" is to present the issues in a way that makes it easy for us to understand. Research has shown that the ability to understand another person's feelings or ideas is a key factor in motivating people to fight racism. Most of us have experienced some form of prejudice, bigotry, or discrimination, and that common bond can reduce racial tension.

Erin A. Oliver, associate director of personnel at the University of Maryland at College Park, is involved with NCBI. He suggests that the most personal and direct method we have to erase racism is to try and understand the thoughts and actions of people of another race. But understanding someone who may hate you because of the color of your skin isn't easy. It takes commitment to reduce your own prejudice and resolve conflicts with others. It takes character not to judge a man by the color of his skin, but by his actions.

Most young people today have been on the front lines of racism and know how hate for another human being can turn deadly. You can make changes in your life by reaching out to people and ideas different from your own, and by taking action when a racial incident occurs.

A TOOL KIT FOR REDUCING RACISM

Here are some things to keep in mind as you work to combat racist attitudes at home, in school, at church, or even on the playground.

(1) Share stories of discrimination. These experiences, often emotion-filled and painful, draw your group together.
(2) Don't make people feel guilty about their racist attitudes. The attempt to erase racism by telling people why they are racist often has the opposite effect.
(3) Develop a sense of control over your own actions. Don't make the other person feel guilty for his or her feelings. Every individual must feel as though he or she can make a difference.
(4) Use humor. Confronting prejudice can be extremely difficult. Don't make it any worse than it has to be. Make every attempt to lighten a tricky subject.

If there is racism in your life, if you are afraid at school or on the streets, if your parents are giving you a hard time about being friends with students of a race different from your own, you can take action. You can make the people in your school and your home face their own prejudices. But you have to start with the most difficult part of that task. You have to start by looking at yourself, and you must resolve to work toward a day when all people of all races are treated fairly and with respect.

When it comes to race, differences need not always divide. You must first be aware of the problem. The mere fact that you're reading this book means you are already on the right path. You must now continue to educate yourself, to become aware, and to be committed to doing the right thing. As Martin Luther King once said, "Now is the time to lift our nation from the quicksands of racial injustice to the solid rock of brotherhood."

Now is the time.

ADDITIONAL RESOURCES

The following organizations are helpful to people who have been discriminated against because of their race, religion, or ethnic background, or to anyone who wants to learn more about racism:

American-Arab Anti-Discrimination Committee, 4201 Connecticut Ave. NW, Ste. 500, Washington, DC 20008 (202) 244-2990.

American Civil Liberties Union, 132 W. 43rd Street, New York, NY 10036 (212) 944-9800.

American Jewish Congress, 15 East 84th Street, New York, NY 10028 (212) 879-4500.

Anti-Defamation League of B'nai B'rith, 823 U.N. Plaza, New York, NY 10017 (212) 490-2525.

Asian American Legal Defense and Education Fund, 99 Hudson Street, New York, NY 10013 (212) 966-5932.

Association of American Indian Affairs, 95 Madison Avenue, New York, NY 10016 (212) 689-8720.

Bureau of Indian Affairs, Department of the Interior, 18th and E Streets NW, Washington, D.C. 20245 (202) 343-1100.

Congress of Racial Equality, 236 West 116th Street, New York, NY 10026 (212) 316-1577.

Hispanic Policy Development Project, 1001 Connecticut Ave. NW, Ste. 310, Washington, DC 20036 (202) 822-8414.

Indian Law Resources Center, 601 E. St. SE, Washington, DC 20003 (202) 547-2800.

Japanese American Citizens League, 1730 Rhode Island Ave. NW #204, Washington, DC 20036 (202) 223-1240.

Martin Luther King Center for Nonviolent Social Change, 449 Auburn Ave., NE Atlanta, Georgia 30312 (404) 524-1956.

National Association of Puerto Rican Civil Rights, 2134 Third Avenue, New York, NY 10037 (212) 996-9661.

National Association for the Advancement of Colored People, 144 West 125th Street, New York, NY 10027 (212) 666-9740.

National Coalition Building Institute, 1835 K Street NW, Ste. 715, Washington, DC 20006 (202) 785-9400.

National Hate Hotline, Department of Justice, Washington, D.C. 20530 (800) 347-HATE.

People United to Save Humanity (Operation PUSH), 930 E. 50th St., Chicago, IL 60615 (312) 373-3366.

FOR FURTHER READING

Arnold, Caroline and Herma Silverstein. *Anti-Semitism: A Modern Perspective.* New York, NY: Julian Messner, 1985.

Ashabranner, Brent. *To Live in Two Worlds: American Indian Youth Today.* New York, NY: Dodd, Mead & Company, 1984.

Bode, Janet. *Beating the Odds.* New York, NY: Franklin Watts, 1991.

Dolan, Edward F. *Anti-Semitism.* New York, NY: Franklin Watts, 1985.

Kranz, Rachel. *Straight Talk About Prejudice.* New York, NY: Facts On File, 1992.

Lester, Julius. *To Be A Slave.* New York, NY: Dial Books for Young Readers, 1968.

McKissack, Patricia and Fredrick. *Taking a Stand Against Racism and Racial Discrimination.* New York, NY: Franklin Watts, 1990.

Mizell, Linda. *Think About Racism.* New York, NY: Walker and Company, 1992.

Pascoe, Elaine. *Racial Prejudice.* New York, NY: Franklin Watts, 1985.

Understanding the Riots (by the staff of the *Los Angeles Times*). Los Angeles, CA: *Los Angeles Times*, 1992.

Glossary

Affirmative Action. A government, school, or business policy that actively seeks to increase the hiring or academic enrollment of members of groups that have experienced discrimination in the past (for example, women and members of minorities).

African-American. A term used to describe a black American who has African ancestry.

Anti-Semitism. Prejudice against Jewish people.

Arab. A term used to describe a person whose ancestry is from the Arab countries.

Apartheid. The name for the official policy of segregation and economic discrimination practiced in South Africa.

Asian. A term used to describe a person who has the characteristics of the people of Asia.

Desegregation. The legally-enforced action of allowing minority groups to share facilities and activities with the majority.

Discrimination. A difference in treatment or favor based on qualities or traits other than merit.

Double Standard. An unwritten policy that applies one set of criteria to one group, and another, tougher standard to another group, that amounts to discrimination.

Ethnicity. The shared customs and cultures of a class or group of people.

Hispanic. A term used to describe a person who has the speech or culture of people of Latin America, Spain, or Portugal.

Iranian. A person who comes from the country of Iran. Also known as a Persian.

Multiculturalism. An emerging academic philosophy that argues for more classroom instruction to include North America's cultural history, and broadening the curriculum to more actively include exposure to the social, scientific, intellectual and artistic contributions of minorities and ethnic groups.

Nationalism. Loyalty and devotion to one nation above all others by emphasizing its culture and interests.

American Indian. A member of any of the earliest peoples of the Western hemisphere, except the Eskimos.

Oppression. Unjust or cruel exercise of authority or power.

Prejudice. A quick judgment of someone based on limited or no information.

Race. A class or kind of people unified by specific characteristics, such as skin color.

Racism. A belief system of advantages based on race, ethnicity, or class.

Racist. Someone who discriminates against people because of their race.

Segregation. The forced separation of people based on their race.

Stereotype. A mental picture that is held in common by a group of individuals that represents an over-simplified opinion or attitude.

INDEX

A

affirmative action programs, 33, 75-77
American Jewish Committee, 52
American Nazi Party, 28, 52 *see also* hate
    groups
Aryan Nation, 43, 44 (pictured) *see also* hate
    groups

B

bias, 17, 33

C

Cato, Gavin, 50
Civil Rights Commission (U.S.), 50
civil rights movement, 33, 61
Cosby, Bill, 37
Crown Heights incident, 50
CURE (Communication Understanding
    Respect Education), 78

D

Denny, Reginald, 56
desegregation, 66-68
discrimination
    affirmative action and, 75-77
    defined, 9
    financial racial, 31 (chart)
    in private clubs, 73
    in restaurants, 33
    reverse, 71
    taking action against, 26, 72, 85
discriminatory practices, 20
Dovidio, (Professor) John, 16-17

E

Elliott, Jane, 21
emigration to the U.S., 5

ethnic
    heritage, 39
    pride, 39-41

F

Farley, John E., 11
Fisher, David, 52, 54
Fletcher, Arthur, 50

H

Harris, Louis, 35
hate
    crimes, 19, 27, 50
    groups, 52-55
Hitler, Adolph, 11
Holocaust, the, 52

K

King, Dr. Martin Luther, 7, 10 (pictured), 11,
    21, 70, 89
King, Rodney, 50, 51, 52, 55, 56 (pictured), 57
Ku Klux Klan, 43, 52, 53 (pictured), 77
    see also hate groups

L

Lapchick, Richard, 34, 73
Los Angeles riots, 50, 55-61

M

majority vs. minority, 14
Malcolm X, 81, 87
Marable, Manning, 41
marriage, interracial, 38
mediator, mediation, 27
minority groups, 14
multiculturalism, 68-70
Murray, (Rev.) Cecil L., 52-54

N

National Coalition Building Institute (NCBI), 83-88
nationalism, 30, 31
Negrete, Louis, 54-55

P

Parks, Rosa, 49
prejudice
   defined, 9
   effects of, 31, 83
   fear and, 15, 19-20
   friendships and, 19
   organized violence and, 50
   racial and cultural, 17, 85

R

race
   physical characteristics of, 11, 13
   relations, 60 (survey)
racial pride, 27-28
racial violence, 50-61, 75
racism
   anecdotes of, 7-8, 11-13, 17-19, 23-26, 29-30,
      32-33, 37-38, 39, 49-50, 65-66, 72-73,
      81-82
   begins at home, 19-20, 37-38
   class and ethnic, 11-13
   classroom solutions to, 26-29, 57-59, 68-72,
      83-89
   confronting, 25-26, 42-43, 75, 83-89
   dating and, 38
   defined, 8-11
   denial of, 21
   discrimination and, 9, 17
   four types of, 11
   free speech and, 43, 45-47, 78-79
   gangs and, 54-55
   in all of us? 16-19
   in school, 65-79
   in sports, 72-75
   lack of control and, 20
   language and, 43
   learned response, 21
   prejudice and, 9, 11
   public accommodations and, 33

results of, 17
teachers and, 71-72
we/they distinction, 17
white Americans and, 16-17
racist(s)
   attitudes, 17, 19, 34-35 (survey),
      40 (survey), 42, 45 (quiz), 82-83, 85
   characteristics, 8
   expressions, 43-45
   in America, percentage of, 17
   psychological superiority, 26
Robinson, Jackie, 72-73, 74
Roosevelt, Eleanor, 23
Rosenbaum, Yankel, 50

S

segregation, 66-67
Skinhead(s), 28, 44 (pictured), 49, 52
   see also hate groups
slaves, slavery, 40-41
stereotypes
   anecdotes of, 14-15
   basis for today's, 17, 85
   breaking, 15-16, 85
   defined, 14
   inventing, 14-15
   reinforced, 14, 17
   toward Arabs, 30
   toward Japanese-Americans, 30
Stern, Kenneth S., 52

T

Taira, Esther, 68, 70
Thoreau, Henry David, 65

U

United Neighborhoods Organization (UNO),
   54

W

Williams, Selase, 43